小井胡同

Small Well Lane

Li Longyun, author of Small Well Lane.

小井胡同

Small Well Lane

A Contemporary Chinese Play
and Oral History

by Li Longyun

Translated and edited by
Hong Jiang and Timothy Cheek

Ann Arbor
THE UNIVERSITY OF MICHIGAN PRESS

Copyright © by the University of Michigan 2002
All rights reserved
Published in the United States of America by
The University of Michigan Press
Manufactured in the United States of America
⊚ Printed on acid-free paper

2005   2004   2003   2002   4   3   2   1

No part of this publication may be reproduced,
stored in a retrieval system, or transmitted in any form
or by any means, electronic, mechanical, or otherwise,
without the written permission of the publisher.

A CIP catalog record for this book is available from the British Library.

Library of Congress Cataloging-in-Publication Data

Li, Longyun, 1948–
   [Xiao jing hu tong. English]
   Small well lane : a contemporary Chinese play and oral history /
Longyun Li ; translated by Hong Jiang, Timothy Cheek.
     p.   cm.
   ISBN 0-472-09795-4 — ISBN 0-472-06795-8 (pbk.)
   I. Jiang, Hong, 1954–   II. Cheek, Timothy.   III. Title.
PL2877.L85 X5313 2002
895.1'252—dc21   2001005533

Contents

Translators' Note	ix
Preface to the English Edition *by Li Longyun*	xi
Introduction: Sense of Place, History, and Community in *Small Well Lane* *by Hong Jiang and Timothy Cheek*	1
Small Well Lane	25
Glossary	135
Bibliography	137

The people's revolution was inspired by sacred beliefs. Because the revolution was great and victorious, the people were uplifted, and worshiped it. But those who threw their lives into revolution—especially the young—received nothing but inexplicable persecution and retaliation, carried out against them in the name of revolution. Was this an absurd tragedy? Was this an experiment that could not be avoided? Was this a universal law of history? Was this worthwhile, or was it a total waste?

—Wang Meng, *Bolshevik Salute*

Translators' Note

Small Well Lane (*Xiaojing hutong,* 小井胡同) was first published in *Drama* (*Juben*) in 1981 and published again in 1985 in the journal *Bell Mountain* (*Zhongshan*), with some revisions in order to accommodate political criticism. Later the play was included in the book *Debates on Small Well Lane* (*Xiaojing fengbo lu*) (Harbin: Heilongjiang Publishing House, 1987). The play was permitted to run for three performances to invited guests only in 1983 and was finally brought to the public in 1985 after several revisions. The play was then cordially welcomed by Beijing audiences and ran consistently for more than one hundred performances to full houses. In 1998 *Small Well Lane* was adapted into a twenty-nine-episode television series for Shanghai TV. The text for this translation, however, is the first version of the play published in *Drama* in 1981. We feel it best reflects the author's intentions. The title carries the many layers of meaning in even the simple things of everyday life. The character *jing* (井) generally means a well, as in a water well. Yet in colloquial usage *jing* also can mean a courtyard (as in *tian jing* 天井) in a traditional four-sided family compound (see "Sense of Place" in the introduction). Since *Xiaojing hutong* has already been discussed in English-language studies as *Small Well Lane,* we have maintained that translation.

Small Well Lane is not Li Longyun's 李龙云 first play, but it is the one by which he has earned his literary prominence. Li Longyun was born in 1948 in Beijing. In 1968, like many urban youth of his generation, he was sent down to a military farm in the Great Northern Wilderness of outer Manchuria to accept reeducation from farmers and soldiers during the Cultural Revolution. He worked there in manual labor for ten years. In 1978, at age thirty, he passed the college entrance exam and entered the Department of Chinese Language and Literature at Heilongjiang University. He studied there for only one year, took the graduate exam, and became a graduate student of Chen Baichen 陈白尘, a well-known playwright and scholar at Nanjing University. He received his master's degree in Dramatic Literature from Nanjing University in 1981 and has been working at Beijing People's Art Theater as a professional playwright since then.

Li Longyun's first literary effort, the poem "A Song in Winds and Rains," appeared in *Chinese Literature* (*Zhongguo wenxue*) in 1972. Since then he has published four one-act plays (*Wash Three Times, The Fan, Profane Society,* and *A Collection of Li Longyun's Humor*), five multi-act plays (*There Is a Small Courtyard, Small Well Lane, Not Far from the Old Summer Palace, Wilderness and Man,* and *Under the Red Banner*), and one television series (*Small Well Lane*). Among them *Wilderness and Man* is another influential work, which has been translated into German and Japanese. His publications also include three novels and some essays on dramatic theories. For a list of Li's works in Chinese, see the bibliography.

We would like to thank all those who have helped us bring this project to fruition. We owe a special thanks to Haiping Yan for encouraging us to undertake this translation. Readers of this play will benefit from reading Professor Yan's introduction and the plays translated in her collection *Theater and Society: An Anthology of Contemporary Chinese Drama* (Armonk, N.Y.: M. E. Sharpe, 1998). She and Mark Selden pushed us to do our best work. We are also grateful to the two anonymous reviewers for the press. Their detailed comments and suggestions have improved what you now see. Our gratitude goes as well to Michigan's perspicacious editors, Ingrid Erickson and Marcia LaBrenz. Finally, we thank Li Longyun for his permission to publish this translation and for his assistance with the photographs.

H.J. and T.C.

Preface to the English Edition

Li Longyun

I grew up in the southern part of the old downtown area of Beijing. The little alley where we lived had a rather civilized name, "the small well." Small well lane was old and crumbling, but in my heart and in my memories it is forever lively, warm, and filled with tenderness. Like a mother, it offered me a gentle breast to rest upon and a strong hand to guide my first steps.... I believe that every writer has a piece of land that his heart calls home, and every hometown has its own unique smell, color, taste, and song. I never stop dreaming of the old arch over the gate made of green brick and the worn down couplets on either side of the gate. I still can hear my grandma's singing, "Little boy, in front of the gate: crying and yelling for a little 'wife,'" and all the beautiful folktales she told me in those summer nights when I slept under the moon and stars. I still remember hiding behind grapevines to wait quietly for the moment when Niu Lang would meet Zhi Nü under the moon when I was five years old.... It is upon such a hometown that a writer's life depends and by which he defies death.

I experienced the historical and political vicissitudes of this lane and shared its happiness and bitterness. I had taught my neighborhood aunties to sing revolutionary songs and helped the uncles to make steel for building our dreamed-for communist paradise. Like many of my childhood friends, I joined the Red Guards to destroy cultural treasures while thinking that we were fighting for the nation and Party.

But no matter how difficult it is to explain our history (perhaps it will never be understood) and how coldly that history used our innocence and faith for various political goals and personal powerplays in the name of revolution, still the common folk of Small Well Lane are the participants and evaluators of history, of its success and its failures. When the nation turns over its old page and begins its new tasks, the people of Small Well Lane are the ones who will again faithfully join that task and run to that new ideal, even though they have been deeply hurt in the past. They are the backbone of the nation! Therefore, I wrote about them and tell their stories. I want everyone to know that there is a Small Well Lane in the southern part of Beijing and that the people who live there have pure and golden hearts.

I have always believed that the people in Small Well Lane understand me, just as I understand them. Thus, there will have to be more stories—the second, third, fourth Small Well Lane.... I am glad to see that American readers are going to meet my friends in Small Well Lane and to listen to their own stories.

Beijing
September 2000

Introduction
Sense of Place, History, and Community in *Small Well Lane*

Hong Jiang and Timothy Cheek

Li Longyun's five-act play *Small Well Lane* (*Xiaojing hutong*) was published in *Drama* (*Juben*) in 1981.[1] With a cast of nearly thirty characters of different social roles and individual persona, the play provides a vivid sense of how a group of working-class Beijing residents living in a courtyard compound on the lane named Small Well experienced China's revolution from 1949 to 1980. It also beautifully records the art of talking and living among Beijing back alley folk. The five acts are set in different historical moments of China: the first on the eve of Beijing's liberation in 1949, the second during the Great Leap Forward of 1958, the third in the beginning of the Cultural Revolution (1966), the fourth just after Mao's death and before the downfall of the Gang of Four (October 1976), and the fifth not long after Deng Xiaoping's success in establishing his new leadership and political policy of intellectual emancipation (*sixiang jiefang*) in 1979–80.

The play opens with a description of the ordinary people in Small Well Lane under the Kuomintang (KMT) Nationalist regime—hungry and anxiously hoping for liberation. They embrace the New China of the Chinese Communist Party (CCP) with great enthusiasm and develop a strong sense of identity with the Party and the nation. They unconditionally throw themselves into the revolution and its political movements, one after another. In return they get nothing but individual and collective loss. They are confused and deeply hurt by the Cultural Revolution and see the downfall of the Gang of Four as a "second liberation." Yet, instead of embracing the second liberation unquestioningly as they had the first liberation, the residents of Small Well Lane assert their right to elect the leadership for their neighborhood committee. The play's ending thus underlines the conclusion that it was the lack of participation in decision making by ordinary people, that is, the lack of normal socialist democracy, that contributed to the economic disaster of the Great Leap Forward and the political nightmare of the Culture Revolution. Therefore, *Small Well Lane* argues, it is time to redefine the meaning of socialist democracy—or, in other words, to reevaluate the relationship between the state and its citizens.[2]

Sense of Place

The five acts of the play all take place in Compound No. 7 of Small Well Lane, an alley, or *hutong,* in Beijing. Beijing's *hutongs* (alleys or lanes) are not only the veins of city life and thoroughfares for traffic but also the site where ordinary people live. They are the primary arenas in which people have experienced the historical, political, and cultural vicissitudes that washed over the capital. If you spend some time wandering through a few of them and chat with those old residents, you will find that each and every *hutong* has its own stories that need to be told. Thus, for many Beijing residents, what is most unforgettable in Beijing? It is the many long and short, wide and narrow, ancient and familiar, lovable and plain, alleys and lanes. Unless one goes back to the lanes, one has not returned home.

The term *hutong* comes from the Mongol language, meaning "well." People could live only where wells were dug. Kublai Khan, the founder of Yuan Dynasty (1260–1368), built his capital in Dadu (the Great City, which became Beijing in 1403 during the Ming Dynasty). The grand-scale construction projects of Dadu began in 1267 and were completed in 1276 with the palaces, offices, neighborhoods, and *hutongs* appearing simultaneously. The capital was built according to the principles set by *Rites of Zhou,* "like a chessboard." According to the *West Jin Gazetteer* (*Xi Jin zhi,* composed by Xiong Mengxing in the last years of Yuan), the main avenues in Dadu, either south-north or east-west oriented, were 24 *bu* (the distance of one step) wide, small ones were 12 *bu,* and *hutong* were 6 *bu* in width. There were a total of 29 *hutongs* when Dadu was built and they increased to 459 in the Ming Dynasty (1368–1644). By 1949, the time of the first act of *Small Well Lane,* there were over 6,000 lanes within the boundary of Beijing, of which 4,550 were located in the inner-city districts. As old Beijing folks say, 360 *hutongs* are given a name, while those without names are beyond calculation, meaning that *hutongs* in Beijing are innumerable.

Between the *hutongs* was land for building residential compounds with inner courtyards. In the Yuan period an allotment of 8 *mu* (about a half-acre) was distributed to officials and merchants willing to move to the new capital to build their homes or businesses. Thus began the grand-scaled formation of Beijing's characteristic residential compounds, the quadrangle *si he yuan*. A *si he yuan* is a four-sided compound with rows of rooms built in the four directions so that a square inner courtyard (sometimes called a *tian jing*) is formed at the center. Such a closed *si he yuan* residence provides a great degree of privacy for a family from outsiders when the only entrance, usually a large wooden gate facing the *hutong*, is shut. Within the four walls, however, might live three or four generations together. Rooms on all four sides have doors opening into the courtyard, so all members of the family can live harmoniously together. For common people often more than one biological family might live together in one *si he yuan*, as in No. 7 compound in *Small Well Lane*. Such a closed compound structure reduced individual family privacy but naturally increased a strong sense of community and community identity among its residents. In addition, in the courtyard trees and flowers can be planted, birds and fish bred; residents can then share the pleasures granted by nature.

According to the theory of *feng shui*,[3] the main entrance of a residence for common people should be at the southeast or northwest corner. Therefore, the *hutongs* of Beijing are mostly east-west oriented, and *si he yuan* line the *hutongs* on both sides with gray walls and gray tiles. *Si he yuan* on the north side of the *hutong* have an entrance on the southeast corner, and those on the south side have it on the northwest corner. As a rule, rooms on the north side of a compound are the principal rooms (*zheng fang*), those on the east and west are called wing rooms (*xiang fang*), and those on the south side of a compound facing principal rooms are called reversed rooms (*dao zuo fang*). The rooms around the courtyard were traditionally assigned according to age and status, with the best rooms (on the north side) going to the most prominent family members, the grandparents. Wing rooms on either side were for the younger generations. *Si he yuan* were generally divided into inner quarters and outer quarters by means of a separating wall built along the southern end of wing

Rooftop view of si he yuan *and alleys.*

rooms on the east and west sides, with a door for residents. Between this separating wall and the south wall of the compound was the outer courtyard. Principal rooms and wing rooms were generally linked by a corridor, a kind of covered porch in front of the rooms that went around the courtyard, providing people with passage and shelter from rain and snow as well as a place to sit and rest and enjoy the harmony of the compound. As the major architectural form of residence in Beijing, *hutongs* and *si he yuan* have existed for several hundred years. They have profound cultural connotations and are the carriers of the art of Chinese living.

There were no *hutong* "street signs" in Beijing until 1934. *Hutongs'* names were simply passed on by word of mouth. When a *hu-*

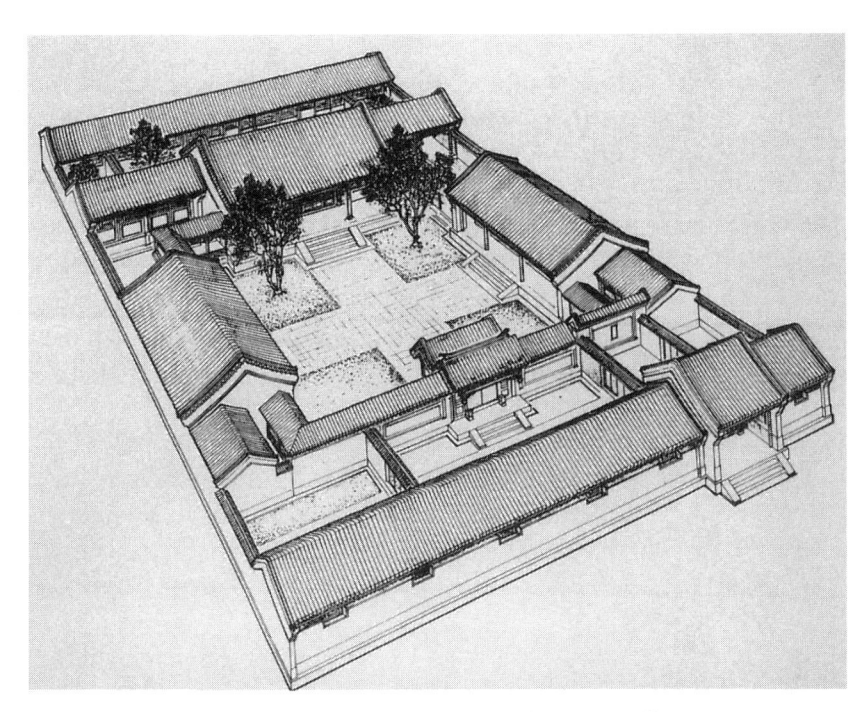

Diagram of a si he yuan *(family compound).*

tong is formed, the residents of that *hutong* will assuredly give it a name that is acceptable to the majority and simultaneously indicates the location and character of the *hutong*. Thus, many were named by their shapes, such as Broad Street for a broader *hutong*, Narrow Lane for a narrow one, One-Foot Alley for a short one, and Bamboo Pole for a long and narrow one. Some names borrowed from well-known city gates, temples, bridges, and wells nearby—for example, Yuan En Temple Alley, Sky Bridge Lane, and Dongzhi Gate Alley. Li Longyun named his lane "Small Well" because he found that there are more than seventy lanes in Beijing that have the character "well" in their names. Thus, Li Longyun's "Small Well" could be a particular name or a general name for any lane in Beijing. The story of the Small Well Lane could also take place in any lane, street, or village in China during those years.

Some *hutongs* took their names from famous people, such as Zhang Zizong, a hero who resisted the Japanese attack at Lugou Bridge in July 1937. Many others were known by the names of notable former residents, such as Kang Youwei, Tan Sitong, Lao She, and

Mao Dun. Some *hutongs'* names have been changed several times over the years, some kept intact since they were first given in the Yuan Dynasty. It is said that about thirty *hutongs* in Beijing have kept their names given in the Ming Dynasty without much change. Furthermore, over a hundred *hutongs* earned their names from their neighborhood stores—for example, Rice Market Lane, Chicken and Duck Market Lane, Fish Market Alley, Coal Lane, Tang-Style Knife Alley, Candle Lane, and Sock Lane. Among the most common stores in these *hutong* neighborhoods were those that sold grain, coal, cotton fabrics, hot water, fruit, wine, snacks, groceries, and other daily necessities. Other shops offered such services as barbering, tailoring, and repair of household items, and there were also teahouses and public bathhouses. Although some of them have actually lost their historical importance in residents' daily life—for instance, Rice Market Lane no longer has a rice market—the old names still prevail because they are closely linked to people's past and *hutong* neighborhood culture.

Wang Zhenqi, a well-known contemporary Chinese author, writes of the contrast *hutongs* provide in a big noisy city:[4]

> Inside the *hutong* it is quiet. Occasionally the sound of the blade-grinder intrudes with a grating clank, or the trill of the blind fortune teller's bamboo flute, or the croaking call of the old wotou-seller, "Haaaaard rolls! Rooooolls!" The timeless sense of "Mountains as peaceful as Antiquity; Days as long as a short year" lives on in these lanes.

Beijing's *hutongs* form an "urban village" that has provided sanctuary and community—and the resilience of daily life—for the capital's many residents. Such urban villages as Small Well Lane provided some refuge for their residents from the political storms of the Mao period. The question remains, however, will the *hutongs* be able to ensure a similar haven for their residents through the storms of commercialization and globalization? Today, many of the old *hutongs* have been torn down and replaced by high-rise offices and apartment blocks. Even Li Longyun's old *hutong* has been built over. Will Beijing's citizens be able to build a new set of urban villages without those twisting lanes?

Li Longyun, the playwright, was born in an ordinary working-class family of Beijing in 1948 and grew up in a little alley that is the

A quiet alley with bicycles.

same as the Small Well Lane he describes in his play. Liu Jiaxiang, the main character of the play, represents his own father, and Grandma Teng and many other characters are portraits of the people he knew so well in his childhood and youth.

Li Longyun himself says:

"What do regular folks want? They only want to live, to live a quiet and stable life in Small Well Lane" (Grandma Teng).

I grew up in the southern part of the old downtown area of Beijing. The little alley where we lived had a rather civilized name, "the small well." Small well lane was old and crumbling, but in my heart and in my memories it is forever lively, warm, and filled with tenderness. Like a mother, it offered me a gentle breast to rest upon and a strong hand to guide my first steps. I believe that every writer has a piece of land that his heart calls home, and every hometown has its own unique smell, color, taste, and song. . . . It is upon such a hometown that a writer's life depends and by which he defies death.[5]

Ernest Gellner calls this the "fatalistic" sense of belonging, namely, an enhanced communal identity in terms of birthplace, natural environment, color, economic condition, common history, and language.[6] It is this communal identity based on place and shared history that forms the heart of *Small Well Lane*. The writer's emotional attachment to his hometown is a constant theme in modern Chinese literature. Fourteen of Lu Xun's twenty-five stories enter a rural world centered on the towns of S (clearly a projection of Lu Xun's hometown, Shaoxing) and Luzhen (his mother's place of origin). Lao She, a novelist and playwright whose name is intimately associated with Beijing, stated in 1935: "Beijing is my hometown. Whenever I think of it, a hundred-foot-long 'panorama of the ancient capital' is shown right before my eyes."[7]

Lao She's well-known play *Teahouse* (*Chaguan*), written in 1957, spans fifty years and has a cast of over sixty characters drawn from all levels of old Beijing society.[8] The strength of *Teahouse*, as critics have argued, is Lao She's familiarity with the characters and language of the streets of the old Beijing he is describing, with its strengths, weaknesses, and ironies. Even though it is affected by political propaganda of 1950s,[9] the play possesses a rich local flavor and provides a unique picture of teahouse culture. It is this local "flavor," Li Longyun believes, that carries *Teahouse* beyond the borders of political propaganda and social criticism and makes it a complex and living work of art. In fact, many critics and dramatists regard Li Longyun's *Small Well Lane* as a continuation of Lao She's *Teahouse* in language, in vision, in unerring choice of significant detail, and in its pronounced emotional attachment to the well-being of the ordinary majority.[10] Like Lao She, whom he greatly admires, Li Longyun is a social playwright, who honestly records the alley in which his characters lived, suffered, and, finally, succeeded.

Beijing is still a focus of interest in recent Chinese films—for example, Mi Jiashan's *Playing for Thrills* of 1988 (based on the popular Beijing writer Wang Shuo's novel *Wanzhu*), Xie Fei's *Black Snow* (1989), and Zhang Nuanxin's *Good Morning Beijing* (1990).[11] These three films indicate different intellectual concerns and cultural criticisms of urban relationships. While *Playing for Thrills* and *Black Snow* draw a dismal picture of the limitations and anxieties of modern city life and the purposeless struggle of individual existence, Zhang's *Good Morning Beijing* expresses the younger generation's desire to participate in the market economy and to create a new urban culture. Although there are different political visions displayed in the three films, they all can be read as a narrative of the birth of urban individualism. Although they differ in their approaches to the image of the city, they all view Beijing as a metropolis or symbolic space in which life is set in an urban complex. *Small Well Lane* contrasts significantly with these films by its sense of place as an ongoing local community of the alley way, not the impersonal bustle of the metropolis, and by its focus on community identity rather than individual identity as an implied solution to the problems of modernization. Tian Zhuangzhuang's *Blue Kite* (1992) appearing ten years after *Small Well Lane*, seems to follow in Li Longyun's footsteps.[12]

Sense of History

It is in this place—one street in the back streets of Beijing—that the people of Small Well Lane experience the political history of China from the 1940s to the early 1980s. Indeed, it is the contrast between the painful experiences of such ordinary people and the grandiose ideals of China's leaders over these decades that gives such power to *Small Well Lane*. Yet the relationship between government ideals and local reality is not simple, nor is it black-and-white.[13] Communist liberation of Beijing in 1949 really does improve the lives of the people in Small Well Lane (see the summary given by Liu Jiaxiang at the start of act 2). Still, the ideological campaigns promoted by Mao—especially the Great Leap Forward and the Cultural Revolution—were unmitigated disasters for them. The impression we are left with is that the Party is good (embodied in the reliable Little Cao, the policeman) but that the radical policies of Mao were mistaken. This is, of course, the CCP's own verdict of 1981 in the famous Central Committee "Historical Resolution."[14] This story line is also captured movingly in Zhang Yimo's well-known movie *Huozhe* (To Live) (and Zhang's movie provides excellent contextual imagery for a class reading *Small Well Lane* while providing an interesting interpretive contrast with its focus on a single family rather than a community).[15]

The CCP came to power in 1949 with considerable popular support after a bitter civil war with the Nationalist government of the KMT. The KMT had been worn out by the Anti-Japanese War (1937–45), while the CCP had developed its policies of people's warfare and land reform during the same years. Ordinary Chinese broadly believed that Chairman Mao's Communists might really deliver the solution to the corruption and inflation of KMT rule. The first decade of CCP rule in China, though not without mistakes, did appear to make good on this promise.

Trouble began in the mid-1950s, when the Party came up with a series of idealistic mass movements that backfired. In reality the top leadership was divided on how best to balance social revolution and economic development. Most important, the CCP had to deal with the unpredictable Supreme Leader they had created in Chairman Mao.[16] From the view of the common person, however, the Party spoke with a single, infallible voice. The policy lurches were thus utterly mystifying. More horrifying, people caught up in the changing policies were blamed for following earlier orders that were later deemed counterrevolutionary.

Three great mass movements typify this tragic pattern. The first was the Hundred Flowers Campaign of 1956–57. The top leadership was seeking ways to protect and promote the interests of ordinary people from the depredations of the huge Leninist bureaucracy the Party itself had created. Mao pushed for more public criticism; the Party leadership anxiously preferred more limited public suggestions. Mao overrode the Party but was horrified when public criticism did not bring him praise but, rather, biting criticism of his rule and suggestions for two-Party democracy! Mao and the Party then agreed that all critics were—despite having answered Party calls to criticize—counterrevolutionaries. Thousands who spoke up to help the Party (as well as those who proposed replacing it) were criticized, denounced as rightists, and sent to virtual prison camps for the next twenty years. This is the fate that befell Qishi'er in *Small Well Lane*. Such people, most of whom were intellectuals loyal to the Party, returned to public life only after the fall of the Cultural Revolution leadership (known now as the Gang of Four) in 1976.

The second great mass campaign was the Great Leap Forward. Following on the heals of the failure of the Hundred Flowers experiment, Mao used this mass movement to harness the strength of China's millions of farmers and workers. The heart of the program was the plan to turn extra labor into industrial capital by means of massive collective projects in farming and "backyard steelmaking." This was a time of incredible euphoria, a sort of collective leaving of one's senses that we see in act 2. As we will suggest, public support of implausible production goals was a form of loyalty that built the new socialist collective identity. In actual fact the economic results of the Great Leap Forward were utter disaster—three years of famine in 1959–61. At the same time as the Party promoted these unrealistic economic goals, and the end of private farming and home cooking in the People's Communes, it also promoted women's rights in the political arena and health care for the very poor through a system of barefoot doctors. The rejection today of the tragic policies of the Great Leap Forward unfortunately also has seen the dismissal of these more noble goals.

The top leadership of the CCP was stricken by the famine caused by the Great Leap Forward, but in public the Leap was declared a success. In the early 1960s, as communities around China tried to recover from the Leap, the top leadership fell into factional fighting. Most of this was out of sight of the average person. Yet it came to a head in the third, and last, great mass campaign under Mao: the Great Proletarian Cultural Revolution. This was an open-ended call by Mao and the Party to youth, and especially students, around China to attack all authority and everything old. Between 1966 and 1968 teenage gangs, called Chairman Mao's "Red Guards," had virtual carte blanche to roam the country (riding for free on the national rail system) and attack whatever they deemed to be counterrevolutionary. The country tottered on the verge of chaos. Local communities, such as Small Well Lane, struggled to make sense of the radical rhetoric and to protect their communities from what appeared to be government-sanctioned random attacks by double-talking teenage gangs. This utter confusion is captured by Shopkeeper Shi in act 3 as he tries pathetically to get the right phrasing for a political "Big Character Poster." The aftermath of the Cultural Revolution left the leadership divided, the charisma of the CCP and its revolution badly tarnished, and local communities around China reeling under a new breed of local tyrants that had come to power during the chaos of the Cultural Revolution. Little Mrs. represents such a radical tyrant in *Small Well Lane*.

The post-Mao period saw first the end of the radical policies of the Cultural Revolution, then some redress of its injustices, and finally a new start at social justice and economic development. Mao died in September 1976. Act 4 of the play takes place during those uncertain weeks after his death and ends with the fateful arrest of the radical leadership under Mao's wife, Jiang Qing. These deposed leftists became the Gang of Four, and they took the blame (instead of Mao) for most of the horrors of the Cultural Revolution. But the changes after Mao did not come easily. We are into act 5 before the change in power—away from the local tyrants and back to some legitimately chosen local leadership—can be consolidated. Certainly, the CCP's ability to effect this change in the early 1980s, including an end to rural communes and the return of land to the tiller, has contributed mightily to its ability to avoid the fate of the Communist Party in the Soviet Union. After all, some twenty years after the fall of the Berlin Wall and the collapse of the Soviet Union, the CCP still rules China.

Li Longyun, himself, has lived this history. He was born in 1948 in Beijing, fifty days before its liberation by the CCP. His life is representative of many Chinese writers of his generation. They grew up with New China during the golden years of China's revolution in 1950s and used to regard themselves as the *tongling ren* (literally "same generation") of the nation. They threw themselves into the Cultural Revolution (1966–76) with all their trust and faith and were proud of being Chairman Mao's Red Guards. They went to the Great Northern Wilderness in 1968 to accept the reeducation of farmers and soldiers under Mao's propaganda of becoming a new revolutionary generation of the nation's educated farmers and workers but soon found that they had been abandoned and sacrificed by the Party and Mao for its political and economic crisis.[17] Facing the tough and hopeless countryside life, many of them at first felt pain and loss and then a sense of being cheated. Finally, they began to question their ideals and even the revolution itself.

In 1978, at age thirty, Li Longyun passed the college entrance exam and entered the Department of Chinese Language and Literature at Heilongjiang University. He studied there for only one year and took the graduate exam and became a graduate student of Chen Baicheng, a well-known playwright and scholar at Nanjing University.[18] *Small Well Lane* was originally written as Li Longyun's thesis for his master's degree in dramatic literature in 1981. Since 1982 Li has been working at Beijing People's Art Theater as a professional playwright.

Thus, as an intellectual coming out of the back streets of Beijing, Li Longyun is like the character Qishi'er in *Small Well Lane*. Qishi'er joined the revolution when he was sixteen and was labeled "rightist" because he offered well-intentioned suggestions in the Hundred Flowers Campaign of 1957. It is he who writes the critical article in act 5 in support of the election of the new neighborhood committee that overthrows the tyrannical Little Mrs. and reconfirms socialist democracy. Li Longyun sets himself up to write on behalf of his street, just as Qishi'er did. And it is from this sense of shared history and community identity, as opposed to modernist alienation, that the heart of Li's play springs.

Sense of Community

Li Longyun suggests an alternative to the new individualism, or "subjectivity," promoted by the debate over socialist humanism in the 1980s. In *Small Well Lane* we see that community-based socialist democracy is not the quest for individual identity as much as an effort at rebuilding community identity. In act 5, after the Cultural Revolution, Small Well Lane's residents elect the new leadership for their neighborhood committee because, on one hand, they realize that it was the lack of a community-based democratic participation in politics that contributed to the disasters they suffered, and, on the other hand, they expect to elect someone who shares their values of living: Auntie Liu, who is hardworking, honest, big-hearted, and speaks for them. For example, Auntie Liu had helped Wu Qi to get his house back from Little Mrs., who illegally took it during the chaos of Cultural Revolution. In a society in which *politics* has for so long meant only a devastating official presence in all aspects of personal life and in which the common people's lives and identities were still mostly centered on community-based neighborhoods, the significance of community identity is fundamental. With its emphasis on loyalty to the family and community, and on individual effort, community identity represents an alternative to collective identity or Party-state identity (with its emphasis on loyalty to the Party-state and on undifferentiated collective effort). Thus, the difference between community identity and collective identity is that, rather than turning people into the collective's or Party-state's "tools," community identity serves the well-being of individuals, their families, and their neighbors. It serves individuals with faces, names, personal histories, and a web of particularistic relationships with family and neighbors. It is not the faceless masses of socialist propaganda that make life but "Aunties," "Third Brothers," and that irritating Shopkeeper Shi whom one cannot live without.

All political campaigns in Mao's China were campaigns of the anonymous masses. For Mao *revolution* was a mass movement that served the collective, instead of the individual.[19] The central questions of this formation of *revolution* are: how does it join individuals into the masses, and how does it affect and transform the sense of self into revolutionary tool? The following "made-up" confession of Chen Jiuling at the meeting of "opening your heart to your leaders" in act 2 probably best illustrates dramatically the nature of such a transformation of the sense of self.

CHEN JIULING: I had a great meeting today! A great meeting! I need a couple of drinks.

SHOPKEEPER SHI: What meeting?

CHEN JIULING: The meeting "to open your heart to your leaders" (*gesturing as he speaks*). There are more than two thousand workers in my company. This one guy had a historical problem; another guy is an active counterrevolutionary.... Confess yourself if you have done anything that makes you feel you let the government down. This is called opening your heart to your leaders! (*covers half of his mouth*). To tell you the truth, most people in my company are the dregs of society. After one person finished confessing his own guilt, the leader walked over to pat him on the shoulders, and the manager shook his hand and encouraged him. I was jealous but had nothing to confess (*enviously*). The leader pats your shoulders! This is no joke! I told myself: Chen Jiuling, this is time to show your dedication! Nothing to confess? Well, make something up! Come on!

Is Chen out of his mind? Or has he simply "taken the wrong medicine," as his concerned neighbors suggest? Otherwise, as Auntie Jiu says, "How can you pour shit on your own head?" Chen Jiuling's concocted confession, indeed, is a natural consequence of the revolutionary self in a time of self-criticism and unconditional dedication to the nation and to the Party. What Chen Jiuling felt in that heat of collective confession was a momentous instant of collective significance, the potential of becoming a part of "the masses." He had no sense of what he was confessing or the consequence of that confession but only one sensuous desire to show his devotion to the Party leaders and to join the collective. This psychic state of total devotion comes close to a sort of religious feeling: total submission to authority.[20] Thus, he does not pause to think or judge; for him the important thing is not what he was confessing but following the words of the authority and the mood of masses.

Obviously, Mao's formation of *revolution* does not simply work as an external form of control; it cannot work without an individual's consent and voluntary partnership. In defining *ideology*, Louis Althusser writes, "What is represented in ideology is not the system of the real relations which govern the existence of individuals, but the imaginary relations of those individuals to the real relations in which they live."[21] Accordingly, as a result of the "imaginary" nature of ideology, all the available representation of the real is always already "necessarily" distorted. Chen Jiuling's cooked up confession is "already necessarily distorted" dedication to the Party leader and the movement of masses. That Chen's confession is so ludicrous only brings tears and laughs of recognition from Li Longyun's audience—so many of whom had made the same mistake.

In her study of the model plays (*yangban xi*) of the Cultural Revolution, Ellen Judd draws the reader's attention to the image of the "dramatic pose" (*liangxiang*): the image of the chief character, Yang Zirong, in *Taking Tiger Mountain by Strategy* (*Zhiqu weihushan*) "posed before a detachment of PLA soldiers and officers against the background of an unfurled red flag or of Li Yuhe in *The Red Lantern* (*Hongdeng ji*) standing upright in blood-stained shirt, striking fear into the hearts of his torturers."[22] Imagine Chen Jiuling standing in front of the leader and his coworkers, confessing his imaginary guilt with all his heart. "I told myself: Chen Jiuling, this is the time to show your dedication! Nothing to confess? Well, make something up! Come on!" It is ironic, but not an exaggeration, to say that it is difficult for us to distinguish Chen Jiuling's dramatic pose from Yang Zirong and Li Yuhe's heroic gestures. Chen Jiuling is, of course, stupid. But his act was a very common reaction of normal people in the collective imagination of Mao's China. Chinese audiences of Li Longyun's generation easily identify with this socialist Forrest Gump. This irony, however, is underlined by tragedy. Unlike the simpleton of the Hollywood movie, Chen Jiuling is turned into the sacrificial victim of the mass movement. He is arrested and sent to a labor farm in northwest China for twenty-two years.

Nonetheless, in the eyes of his neighbors in Small Well Lane, Chen Jiuling was, is, and will continue to be their Little Jiu, whom they have known for years in their daily lives not as an "advanced element" nor as a "revolutionary enemy" but simply and powerfully as their friend and neighbor. In his definition of the significance of existence in the "everyday," Henri Lefebvre argues: "the everyday is a *product*. . . . The everyday is therefore the most universal and the most unique condition, the most social and most individuated, the most obvious and the best hidden."[23] For Lefebvre "the everyday is covered by a surface: modernity"; for Li Longyun the everyday is covered by Mao's vision of the "revolution" or the mass movement. The collective movement created not only its own model plays and slogans but also an imagined way of life that took people away from their "normal" sense of themselves and their everyday living. *Small Well Lane* thus emphasizes the significance of the everyday-based neighborhood community identity as the underlying reality that survives and succeeds revolution.

For Mao Zedong revolution was a drama or collective performance filled with spectacles. In a conversation with the French writer André Malraux, Mao said, "Revolution is a drama of passion; we didn't win the people over by appealing to reason, but by developing hope, trust and fraternity."[24] How can revolution be a "drama of passion" and promoted through "developing hope, trust and fraternity"? Slavoj Žižek's writing after the collapse of communism in Eastern Europe suggests an answer in the "nation-Thing":

> The Thing is not directly a collection of these features [composing a specific way of life]; there is "something more" in it, something that is *present* in these features, that *appears* through them. Members of a community who partake in a given "way of life" *believe in their Thing* . . . : "I believe in the (national) Thing" is equal to "I believe that others (members of my community) believe in the Thing."[25]

The power of revolution, in this view, lies not so much in its reason or truth but in *believing in their Thing*.

Such collective blind faith and hope is built on unconditional "sacrifice." In act 2, during the Great Leap Forward movement of

1958, Small Well Lane residents, like everyone in China at that time, were involved in the social fantasy of digging out iron to make steel for building a communist paradise in China. Thus, following a rumor that abandoned cannons from the Qing Dynasty might be buried under Compound No. 7, the residents there decided to tear down the very houses in which they lived. The play does not tell the audience if such a sacrifice was worthwhile or not. The issue here is not the existence or nonexistence of abandoned cannons but the sacrifice itself. As Liu Jiaxiang, the main character, claims: "Elder Brother Shi [the owner of that house and most of Compound No. 7], don't hesitate! The government needs our support [or sacrifice] now. Let's be fair. Have we ever seen such a good government before?!" The act of digging cannons is thus a signifier that constitutes the collective identity demanded by the Party-state through its call for unconditional trust. Through such acts people could escape their everyday common sense and *believe* without question what Little Cao, the policeman, reports—that "15,000 lbs. of grain was grown in one *mu*. It is said that children can play on top of the grain stalks and won't fall in."

Small Well Lane's common folk "falsely" hold the belief that tearing down a house (as an act of loyalty) will bring them a national paradise. "Eat at the dinning hall and live in the high-rises. Communism stands before us!" they say in act 2. This emotional hope is a predominant feature of the Great Leap Forward and most of the other mass movements in modern China. Mao's personality cult gradually reached a peak of unconditional worship of himself and the masses in the Cultural Revolution (1966–76). Finally, not only intellectuals but also Party leaders and ordinary workers (who for years had been thought of as the beneficiary of the revolution) themselves all became victims. The power of Li Longyun's *Small Well Lane* is its ability to take the audience sympathetically into this madness and then to redeem us and the ordinary, fallible people of that lane (who, after all, *are* us) through common, everyday community life. Li Longyun thus humanizes not only the great problem of the Chinese revolution but its solution as well.

Twists and Turns in the Life of *Small Well Lane*

In the late 1970s and early 1980s there was a group of writers in China who called themselves the school of critical realism. They proclaimed that the essential function of theater is to make social criticism. These critical realists declared an emotional attachment to the ordinary Chinese and to their daily experiences.[26] *Small Well Lane* caught the attention of these critics and dramatists almost overnight after its publication. A group of prominent directors and actors at Beijing People's Art Theater contacted Li Longyun and decided to produce the play in 1981.

Not long after earning literary prominence, Li Longyun found himself and his *Small Well Lane* a target of the Campaign against Spiritual Pollution of 1983 and 1984.[27] The Party critics argued that the play focused on such economic and political mistakes as the Great Leap Forward and the Cultural Revolution. "It seems as if the Great Leap Forward and the Cultural Revolution were the only two things that we [the Communist Party] have done since liberation—such a representation of PRC history appears rather lopsided."[28] Some complained that the play depicted people's lives in Mao's China as even harsher than in old Beijing's society under the KMT. In China's official discourse it is generally assumed that the society before liberation was a "dark age." Under the leadership of the CCP in New China it is believed that the people were striding forward toward a better life and brighter future in a long march toward "communism" (replaced by "modernization" in the post-Mao period). The question at the core of this controversy is, obviously, how to reevaluate China's convoluted revolution and how to represent some of the most critical political moments of the nation since 1949.

The play was staged in the summer of 1983 but was permitted to run for only three performances to invited guests. Li Longyun remarks, however: "I don't know what the critics will say about *Small Well Lane*. Indeed, I don't care about their opinions. What truly concerns me are the comments of the folks who live in Small Well Lane. They are my critics and conscience!"[29] The shift of political winds forced him to revise some parts of the play and to create a brighter ending. Li Longyun sighs, explaining that he created two versions of act 1 and four of act 5 for *Small Well Lane* between 1983 and 1985. (The present translation, however, is of his original 1981 version of the play without the later revisions.)

In spring of 1985 the revised play was finally brought to the public after these revisions and three years' bitter controversy involving playwrights, dramatists, critics, and members of the Party's cultural administration. The play was a success, running consistently for more than one hundred performances to full houses, creating a box office record for Beijing People's Art Theater at a time when modern spoken drama had been losing its audience to film and television.[30] Li Longyun owed his popularity to the fact that audiences readily identified with his characters. In his play they saw their own art of living, their own sufferings and struggles, and their own unconditional devotion to the revolution. The audiences were attracted not only by Li Longyun's ability to grapple with these crucial problems of the day but also by his masterful recreation of the characters and language of Beijing alleys as well as by his effort to be a voice for the "voiceless" common man and woman.

While *Small Well Lane* was welcomed by its Beijing audience, it was not appreciated by a group of modernist playwrights and dramatic critics who favored the quest for "modern subjectivity" in the mid-1980s. This group of modernists declared that art in its essence was independent of politics, not representing any socioeconomic group or class. They rejected the critical realism of Li Longyun and his colleagues. They judged the socialist ethics—the collective well-being of the working people—offered in *Small Well Lane* as hackneyed and outdated, really just another variant of "ideological orthodoxy."[31] According to Haiping Yan, the appearance of *Small Well Lane* looked tragically out-of-date on the fast-changing cultural scene of 1985. By then "Chinese modernism" had identified not only with decollectivization of the rural economy but with the partial denationalization or internationalization of the urban economy. Literature and art "were expressions of individual subjectivity endowed with universal humanity."[32] Thus, just as *Small Well Lane* was finally brought to the public after a three-year effort at pleasing conservative Party critics, it was immediately criticized by cultural liberals. If the play had earlier been criticized as misleading audiences' understanding of China's socialist revolution, it now as faced the charge of promoting an outdated community-based socialist democracy.

Li Longyun responded to this criticism of experimental modernism in his interview with an American journalist in 1985:

> What's most attractive about a writer is his or her own character, and what is most appealing about a nation is its own cultural spirit and form of living. . . . A play is significant internationally if it is characterized by its own unique artistic style and resonates with its own profound cultural traditions. I believe that our pro-

ductions of plays like *Rhinoceros* and *Bald Soprano* cannot surpass the productions by Western theater companies, but I dare say that there is no theater in the entire world that can produce a better production of *Teahouse* than the Beijing's People's Art Theater Company.[33]

It is for just this reason—its own form of living and its own profound cultural tradition—that *Small Well Lane* has been staged for the public three times, in 1983, 1985, and 1993, by Beijing People's Art Theater and has appeared on national television in 1998 (see bibliography for details).

We are delighted to bring the community of Small Well Lane to English readers in this edition. Along with this introduction, we have added a glossary as well as ten photographs to help readers new to China to appreciate the world in which these characters live. We have also included a short bibliography of English works for our new friends and a Chinese bibliography for our old friends. Our goal, however, is the same as Li Longyun's—to bring you into the world of Small Well Lane.

NOTES

1. The monthly journal *Juben* has been the authoritative forum of the theater world in China since 1952. See our translation note and bibliography for publication details.

2. See Haiping Yan, *Theater and Society: An Anthology of Contemporary Chinese Drama* (Armonk, N.Y.: M. E. Sharpe, 1998), ix–xv, for more comments.

3. *Feng shui*, or geomancy, is the traditional Chinese practice of physical orientation of buildings, and especially graves, to promote the beneficial flow of natural forces (*qi*) in order to bring or maintain good fortune. For more details, see Ronald G. Knapp, *China's Living Houses: Folk Beliefs, Symbols, and Household Orientation* (Honolulu: University of Hawaii Press, 1999).

4. Wang Zhenqi, "Gudu can meng—hutong" (Hutongs—Dreams from the Old Capital), in *Hutong jiushijiu* (Ninety-nine Hutongs), ed. Cheng Xiaoling (Beijing: Beijing Publishing House, 1996), no. 19.

5. Li Longyun, "A Conversation with an American Journalist on the Occasion of the Revival of the Play, *Small Well Lane*, on March 4th, 1985" (*Jiu "Xiaojing hutong" congxing huifu yanchu he Meiguo jizhe de tanhua*), *Yingju yuekan* (July 1985): 7. The English version is based on Haiping Yan's translation in *Theater and Society*, with some revisions.

6. See Ernest Gellner, *Nations and Nationalism* (Ithaca, N.Y.: Cornell University Press, 1983), 61–62.

7. Quoted from Yingjin Zhang, *The City in Modern Chinese Literature and Film* (Stanford: Stanford University Press, 1996), 61. The "panorama" to which Lao She refers is the famous hand scroll of Kaifeng, the capital of the Song Dynasty, which pictures all the activities of daily street life.

8. The English edition of *Teahouse* was published in 1980 by Foreign Languages Press, Beijing, China. The Chinese video is available in the United States with English subtitles.

9. Colin Mackerras remarks that the play "is not intending to tell a story as much as to depict the deterioration and corruption" of the old Beijing and Kuomintang officials (*Chinese Drama* [Beijing: New World Press, 1990], 155–56).

10. See Dong Jian, "From *Small Courtyard* to *Small Well Lane*," *Xinhua Monthly,* no. 7 (1979); and Chen Baichen, "Reread *Small Well Lane*," in *Debates on Small Well Lane* (Heilongjiang: People's Publishing House, 1987), 51–59.

11. All of these videos are available with English subtitles. A good source for Chinese videos is China Film Import & Export (L.A.) Inc./A China Film Export & Import Corporation Company, 2500 Wishire Blvd., No. 1028, Los Angeles, CA 90057.

12. The film *Lan fengzheng* is also available as a video with English subtitles.

13. An excellent general history of this period that gives due attention both to the ideals of the Party and the suffering of the people is Maurice Meisner, *Mao's China and After* (New York: Free Press, 1986).

14. The post-Mao resolution was passed by the CCP CC on June 27, 1981, and published widely. It finds it authoritative interpretation in the Document Research Office of the CCP CC, ed., *Guanyu jianguo yilai dangde ruogan lishi wenti de jueyi zhushiben (xiuding)* (Annotations, Revised Edition, of the Resolution on Certain Historical Questions of the Party since the Founding of the Nation) (Beijing: Renmin chubanshe, 1985); the resolution itself is reprinted on pages 3–71. The *Beijing Review* published the official English version in its July 6, 1981, edition, which is reprinted, along with useful analysis, in Helmut Martin, *Cult and Canon: The Origins and Development of State Maoism* (Armonk, N.Y.: M. E. Sharpe, 1982), 180–231.

15. Zhang Yimo's film *Huozhe* (To Live) is available in video with English subtitles. It is a long and violent film, reminiscent in some ways of a *Dr. Shivago* but more focused on family values rather than romance.

16. The best studies of this political history are Roderick MacFarquhar's three volumes of *Origins of the Cultural Revolution* (New York: Columbia University Press, 1974, 1983, 1997); and Frederick Teiwes, *Politics and Purges in China,* 2d ed. (Armonk, N.Y.: M. E. Sharpe, 1993).

17. A good memoir of this experience, especially of idealistic youth working in the Great Northern Wilderness of Manchuria, is Rae Yang, *The Spider Eaters* (Berkeley: University of California Press, 1996). A fine overview of the Cultural Revolution from a post-Mao perspective is in Yan Jiaqi and Gao Gao,

Turbulent Decade: A History of the Cultural Revolution, ed. and trans. D. W. Y. Kwok (Honolulu: University of Hawaii Press, 1996).

18. Chen Baichen 陈白尘 (1908–) began participating in theater and film groups in Chengdu and Chongqing during the War of Resistance to Japan in 1940s. He wrote a series of satirical plays, among them *Men and Women in Wild Times, The Wedding March,* and *Plan for Promotion.* After the Cultural Revolution he finally completed his historical play *Song of the Wind.* (See glossary for Chinese characters.) As of 1979, he was teaching at Nanjing University and serving as vice chairman of the Playwrights' Association. An English translation of *Men and Women in Wild Times* is included in *Twentieth-Century Chinese Drama: An Anthology,* ed. Edward M. Gunn (Bloomington: Indiana University Press, 1983), 126–73.

19. As Mao proclaims: "Revolutionary culture is a powerful revolutionary weapon for the broad masses of the people. It prepares the ground ideologically before the revolution comes and is an important, indeed essential, fighting front during the revolution." Quoted from *The Selected Works of Mao Tse-tung* (Beijing: Foreign Languages Press, 1965), 1:308.

20. This aspect of CCP rule is analyzed in Teiwes, *Politics and Purges,* chap. 1, and captured emotionally in Rae Yang, *Spider Eaters.*

21. Louis Althusser, "Ideology and Ideological State Apparatuses," in *Lenin and Philosophy and Other essays,* trans. Ben Brewster (New York: Monthly Review Press, 1980), 127–86.

22. Ellen Judd, "Dramas of Passion: Heroism in the Cultural Revolution's Model Operas," in William Joseph et al., eds., *New Perspectives on the Cultural Revolution* (Cambridge, Mass.: Harvard University Press, 1991). The role of the "heroic aesthetic" is well analyzed in Ban Wang, *The Sublime Figure of History* (Stanford: Stanford University Press, 1997).

23. Henri Lefebvre, "The Everyday and Everydayness," *Yale French Studies* (1987): 73, 79.

24. Quoted from Judd, "Dramas of Passion," 265.

25. Slavoj Žižek, "Eastern Europe's Republics of Gilead," *New Left Review* 183 (September–October 1990): 53. In *The Sublime Object of Ideology* (London: Verso, 1989), p. 126, Žižek argues, "Fantasy is a means for an ideology to take its own failure into account in advance."

26. See Haiping Yan, "Introduction," in *Theater and Society.* Yan points out playwrights such as Zong Fuxian, Zhong Jieying, Yao Yuan, Li Jie, and Li Longyun loosely gathered under the banners of the school of critical realism.

27. On intellectual politics in the 1980s, see Merle Goldman, Timothy Cheek, and Carol Lee Hamrin, eds., *China's Intellectuals and the State: In Search of a New Relationship* (Cambridge, Mass.: Harvard University Press, 1987).

28. Archivists of *Juben,* "Regarding the Debates on Several Spoken Dramas" (*Guanyu ji ge huaju de zhengyi*), *Juben* (Drama) (February 1985): 7. Quoted in Haiping Yan, *Theater and Society,* xii.

29. Quoted from *Debates on Small Well Lane* (Heilongjiang: People's Publishing House, 1987), 12.

30. In 1983, 87 percent of the households in Beijing and Shanghai had television sets, and, from that year on, more than one hundred new films were released annually. For more information, see Huang Weijun's "My Thoughts on Spoken Drama's Future" (*Wo dui huaju qiantu zhi duanxiang*), *Xijubao* (July 1983): 34. Quoted in Haiping Yan, *Theater and Society,* xxvii.

31. Quoted from Haiping Yan, *Theater and Society,* xxxi.

32. Ibid., xxxii. For an excellent study of these trends, see Xudong Zhang, *Chinese Modernism in the Era of Reform* (Durham, N.C.: Duke University Press, 1997).

33. Li Longyun, "A Conversation with an American Journalist," *Film and Drama Monthly* (July 1985): 8. Quoted in Haiping Yan, *Theater and Society,* xxxii. The interview was held on March 4, 1985, at Beijing People's Art Theater.

Small Well Lane

by Li Longyun

Translated by Hong Jiang and Timothy Cheek

*The old neighbors all said,
wouldn't it be wonderful if
Small Well Lane could
have a storyteller
to tell their story . . .*

CHARACTERS

(Ages given are those at first appearance)[1]

GRANDMA TENG   Widow of the poor but well-known martial arts expert Teng Fengshan. Born in Beijing in 1898, she is a living historical monument for Small Well Lane.[2]

THIRD SON WATER   Male, in his thirties. Continues the family water delivery service. Studied martial arts with Teng Fengshan as a devoted and loyal student.

WU QI   Male, in his thirties. Sergeant in the Nationalist government (Kuomintang [KMT]) police force. Greasy, timid, but goodhearted.

BI WU   Male, forty years old. Cruel and malicious. Born into a family that dealt in selling women and children. His father, Old Bi Wu, had a monopoly during the Qing Dynasty to supply eunuchs for the Imperial Palace (Forbidden City).

LIU JIAXIANG   Male, over thirty. At age fourteen he had gone to work at the Trolley Bus Factory, where he was an apprentice of Teng Fengshan.

AUNTIE LIU   Thirty-something, given name Fengzhen. Wife of Liu Jiaxiang. Upright and fair-minded, a bit superstitious, softhearted, but sharp-tongued.

ELDER BROTHER "SCARRED SQUINT"   Male, eighteen years old. Orphaned as a teenager. Lives by himself and earns his living by making candy figurines.

ER NIU   Eight years old. Daughter of Liu Jiaxiang. The best friend of Elder Brother "Scarred Squint." Proper name: Liu Guiying.

LITTLE STURDY[3]   Five years old. Adopted son of Liu Jiaxiang. Orphaned child of an executed CCP couple. Auntie Liu, fearing he would not live to maturity, prayed at the temple and received a Buddhist name for him: Seng Bao, literally "Blessed by the Sangha."

MA DEQING   Male, over forty. Old servant of the Wei Family. Kindhearted.

QISHI'ER[4]   Male, sixteen. Child bought by the Wei Family and later formally adopted by their servant Ma Deqing.

XU SIX   Male, over thirty. Craftsman making a living by knitting socks. Chicken-hearted, obliging, good-for-nothing.

SPRING HAPPINESS   Former low-class prostitute in her twenties. Second wife of Xu Six. Not a bad person but often tortured by excessive anxieties.

LITTLE NI'ER   Nine years old. Xu Six's first wife's daughter. Taken in by Liu Jiaxiang and his wife, she changed her name to Liu Guizhi.

SHOPKEEPER SHI   Personal name, Ruifeng. Thirty-something. Runs a grain shop. Astute, worldly-wise, a little selfish, but a good person.

AUNTIE SHI   Thirty-something. Mistress of the Shi Family shop. Illiterate but reckons herself quite intelligent. Often used by others as a weapon or tool.

FORTUNE-TELLER YANG   Male, forty. Fortune-teller who changed his career to selling New Year's paintings.

LITTLE RING   Male, twenty-five. Sells fake medicines. Greedy, lazy, shameless.

LITTLE LIBEN   Male, seventeen. Shop assistant to the Shi Family. Decent, without ambition.

LITTLE MRS.   Family name, Zhou. Twenty-something. The wife of Little Liben. A political schemer. Will rise to the powerful position in the neighborhood committee.

CHEN JIULING   Male, over twenty. Apprentice of Shopkeeper Shi. Formerly compelled to serve the KMT as a cook. Uneducated. A good fellow and better talker.

AUNTIE JIU   Wife of Chen Jiuling, in her twenties. Goodhearted, dutiful, but indecisive.

LITTLE CAO   Male, twenty-something. District policeman for Small Well. Later promoted to district chief. Upright, compassionate.

BIG OX   Son of Chen Jiuling, born in 1954. A "Class of '70" high school graduate.[5]

BIG HORSE   Male, twenty. A Red Guard in a small street factory making woolen knitwear. In 1976 becomes a member of the Workers' Militia.[6] Looks stupid but in reality gets what he wants.

ZENG FU   Male, twenty-five. Nephew of Shopkeeper Shi. Sells fish at the market. Honest, dependable.

LITTLE SIX NINE   Male, born in 1966. Son of Er Niu (Liu Guiying); grandson of Liu Jiaxiang.

Old courtyard gate.

ACT ONE

TIME January 21, 1949, the thirty-eighth year of the Republic. The twenty-third day of the twelfth month in the lunar calendar, popularly known as the "Kitchen God Day."[7] Around dinnertime, 5 P.M.—the time when the Kitchen God will ascend to Heaven.

The eve of the peaceful liberation of Beiping.[8]

PLACE Beiping, Small Well Lane.

SCENE This is a little lane that runs north-south. Going to the right, the south end of the lane runs into the Goddess Temple.[9] To the left, at the north end of the lane, is a small market. The middle of the lane makes a U-bend, which goes around a small open rectangle. Don't look down on this small arena! During peacetime on a winter evening *wanton* sellers, cooked lamb's feet peddlers, fried tofu sellers, and sausage sellers can't help but settle their carrying poles in this square and hawk their wares! In summer the old *Chun* tree[10] growing above the square gives the old neighborhood the great benefit of its umbrella that casts a large cool shadow. People nursing their rice bowls gather under the tree and pour out their difficulties and troubles. . . .

In the middle of the lane is Compound No. 7. Here live working-class city folk. The arch over the gate made of green brick and tile in the Five Flower Petal style is already broken and crumbling. The antithetical couplets carved on either side of the gate have long been worn down by the winds and rains so that one can hardly read them: "When drawing up plans, allow for the unforeseen; / Apply your mind, and your life will be at ease." Inside the compound is a broken screen wall.

On the right side of the compound there appears a small door. Above the door frame is hung a porcelain plaque: *House of Wei*. This back door of the Wei household hasn't been used for who knows how many years. But now the little door opens! When the Eighth Route Army[11] surrounded Beiping like an iron band, the House of Wei was thrown into confusion!

Not far away, at the temporary airport at the Temple of Heaven,[12] airplanes take off and land like flies—in addition to the transports dropping supplies—buzzing ceaselessly throughout the day. The great cannons of the Eighth Route Army are trained directly at this airport, preventing any chance of escape. Everyone in Small Well Lane is anxious. The poor sensed it: were their days of hardship nearly over? They longed for the Eighth Route Army to enter the city as soon as possible, but, on the other hand, they hoped the army would not open fire—Beiping, after all, is an ancient capital!

> [CURTAIN RISES. *The buzzing sound of airplanes gradually fades. Through the distant sound of cannon a desolate voice hawking Guangdong candy floats from the north entrance of the lane:* "Candy for sale, Guangdong candy for sale!" *From the southern courtyard rises the sound of firecrackers sending the Kitchen God to heaven, but there are only a few pops, which fail to create a celebratory atmosphere.*
>
> [*With his left hand* Liu Jiaxiang *holds a picture of the Kitchen God that he has peeled from the stove; in his right hand he carries a punk as he walks through the courtyard door. This is a man who doesn't know the meaning of anxiety, but over the past few days even he can't keep calm! He is so hungry that his stomach has begun to dominate his mind . . .*
>
> Sergeant Wu Qi *emerges from the southern entrance of the lane, holding a dozen strips of red paper.*]

LIU JIAXIANG (*immediately sees* Wu Qi): Master Qi! Master Qi (*walking over*), Are people saying Fu Zuoyi[13] shook hands with the Eighth Route Army? Then how come there was gunfire all night outside the Qihua Gate three nights ago?

WU QI (*looking all around and lowering his voice*): That was at the water works, the 208th Division mutinied! They've broken with Fu Zuoyi . . .

LIU JIAXIANG: Those lackeys . . .

WU QI: Elder Brother Liu, haven't you heard? The Eighth Route Army thinks Fu Zuoyi can't control his army. They've asked for Xizhi Gate to be opened to let two divisions of the Eighth Route Army enter the city under Fu Zuoyi's command . . .

LIU JIAXIANG: Well, they are gracious. But how about Fu Zuoyi?

WU QI: Fu Zuoyi? He can't be vague (*half-covering his mouth with his hands*). The 208th Division has been eliminated . . .

[*Just then the sounds of a hoarse voice singing a Beijing folk song, "Song of Great Peace," waft over from the north entrance of the lane.*]

December 23rd, send the spirit to Heaven; speaking of
human kindness and evil.
The head of the house kneels down; holding
burning incense . . .

[*A hawking voice: "Pictures! Pictures for sale!"*
The fortune-teller Yang Banxian *comes out of the north entrance wearing an undersized cotton jacket. With one hand he covers his frozen ear; with the other he grasps a roll of New Year's pictures.*]

WU QI: What? Yang Banxian, have you stopped telling fortunes?

FORTUNE-TELLER YANG (*using his sleeve to wipe his runny nose*): Sergeant Wu, you are a sage. This year, the rich don't believe in fate, they believe in this! Yankee dollars! Silver dollars! The poor haven't a single penny in their pockets. Elder Brother Liu, lend a hand, buy a picture. It's Yangliuqing, a real Tianjin product.[14] (*Unrolling the pictures*) How about this one. "Celebrate and Enjoy a Harvest Year" . . .

LIU JIAXIANG: Celebrate and Enjoy a Harvest Year? Heh, heh. This stomach of mine is full of bean curd dregs . . .

FORTUNE-TELLER YANG: . . . This one, take a look at this one. "He Rides a Fine Horse; I Ride a Donkey" . . .

LIU JIAXIANG (*giving the painting a once-over*): Take a look at that little donkey. The meat on that leg is so firm. But Master Qi, no matter how I look at it, this little donkey still isn't enough for one meal . . .

FORTUNE-TELLER YANG: What are you saying! Okay, okay, you're hungrier than me (*rolls up the picture*). Elder Brother Liu, I give in. (*Sings in a soprano voice*):

> Head of the house kneels down, holding burning incense
>   in his hand.
> Don't ask for wealth and treasure; don't ask for food
>   and clothes.
> Speak my good and hide my wrongs.

[*Sings as he walks away. The sound gradually fades.*]

LIU JIAXIANG: Master Qi, guess where I went. I went to Beihai Park. On the off chance that the transports might drop a bag of supplies nearby.

WU QI: In this turmoil and chaos of war you really know how to get your kicks . . .

LIU JIAXIANG: We think coarse *wotou* buns are gold ingots; they (*pointing at the small door*) take the best American white flour and toss it around like dirt . . .

WU QI: White flour? Elder Brother Liu, they have much better—combination hotpot from Bianyi Restaurant, Suzhou cakes, palace-style chestnut patties . . .

LIU JIAXIANG: Why? Master Qi, why can they wine and dine while our stomachs growl? The Eighth Route Army stays too calm. If their mortars just began firing and they put up the ladders, they would have long since had Beiping in their hands . . .

[Auntie Liu *comes out of the courtyard leading* Little Sturdy.]

AUNTIE LIU (*to* Little Sturdy): Slowly, that's a good boy, watch out. Oh! Sergeant Wu . . . (*sees the picture of the Kitchen God in* Liu Jiaxiang's *hand*). Is there anyone offering a sacrifice on the street? What good are you!

LIU JIAXIANG: Haven't you heard the cannons? The house could collapse and bury me!

AUNTIE LIU: Don't be such a scaredy-cat, you are not some precious wine cup. The Eighth Route Army cannons have eyes; they don't blow up poor people.

WU QI: Auntie Liu, you . . . this . . .

AUNTIE LIU: We're going up to the Goddess Temple to get a blessing for Little Sturdy . . .

LIU JIAXIANG: You're always coming up with harebrained ideas! You pierced Eldest Son's ear, and did he live? (*To* Wu Qi) When it came to our second child, who was obviously a boy, she persisted in calling him "Missy Liu"[15] (*lowering his voice*). In addition, Little Sturdy is not our natural-born son, so his fate isn't as bad as ours.

AUNTIE LIU: It's New Year's Eve—I'm not going to quarrel with you. Sergeant Wu, you know (*lowers her voice*) this child has no father or mother. When I look at him, I feel so sad. They insisted on saying his parents were in the Eighth Route Army, and so . . . executed! (*Suddenly remembers*) Sergeant Wu, did I hear that this is the child you carried out of jail and placed at the entrance of the lane?

WU QI: Auntie Liu! Auntie Liu! Don't say that! Don't say that! Okay? (*draws his hand across his throat in a slash*). You don't want my head cut off? (*hurriedly holds up the red slips in his hand*). All right. I still have some formal business to do. Commissioner Ding—Big head Ding's old mother is turning seventy, I've gotta collect birthday contributions . . .[16]

LIU JIAXIANG (*anxiously*): Collecting birthday contributions again?

WU QI: Old motherfucker. Before leaving he wants to get another "serving." So he picked up an old lady off the street and declared she was his mother, turning seventy. Who dares not to contribute? Who would dare? His son is commander of the 208th Division, in good with the secret police[17] . . . but the culprit is always me . . . (*slides a red contribution slip into* Liu Jiaxiang's *hand*).

AUNTIE LIU: Sergeant Wu, we know your difficulty. (*To* Liu Jiaxiang) Don't worry about the contribution. Just take the card! (*In a loud voice*) Er Niu! Er Niu! (*To* Liu Jiaxiang) You go get Er Niu, don't let her be kidnapped. Little Sturdy, good boy, come with mama . . . (*To* Liu Jiaxiang) You haven't prepared straw and beans for the spirit horse? The Kitchen God is not like you; he needs to ride his horse to get around. You're not performing the ceremony; you're fooling me!

WU QI: Auntie Liu, men don't pray to the moon; women don't sacrifice to the Kitchen God. Go do your business . . .

[*Auntie Liu leads* Little Sturdy *out the south end of the lane. Along with the "ggh-ggh" sound of cart wheels,* Third Son Water, *with pads on his shoulders and towels on his shins, comes pulling a water cart from the north end of the lane.* Third Son Water's *name, like his job, is hereditary. The body of the cart is one large, wooden, egg-shaped box; behind and below the frame is the water tap.*]

THIRD SON WATER (*puts down the bucket, fills it, and totes it to the courtyard gate*): Water! (*Being nearsighted, he presses his nose to the gate post, pulls out his chalk, and adds a stroke to delivery marks.*)

WU QI: Third Son Water, is the price of water going up, too?

THIRD SON WATER (*pointing to the white marks on the door post*): Do you see this? One mark, one delivery. The old neighborhood is so poor it can't even pay for water! Look at all these chicken scratches—it just makes me want to cry! How could it come to this . . . ? (*enters the courtyard*).

[Xu Six *walks out of the gate. He is wearing a fairly new dark-blue gown. But it's tight and squeezes his body no matter how much he tugs and pulls at it. And it's too short to cover the rim of his worn cotton underclothes.*]

XU SIX: Elder Brother Liu, will you keep an eye out for me? My little daughter is sleeping on the *kang*.[18] I'm taking advantage of the dark . . . so people won't peek . . .

WU QI: You're going . . . (*realizes*) Oh! Okay. So you won't always be thinking of your wife . . . feeling sad . . .

LIU JIAXIANG: Xu Six, aren't you going to have a wedding party?

XU SIX (*with a sad smile*): You shouldn't tease me, bringing home an ex-hooker . . .

LIU JIAXIANG: Even she should be introduced to the old neighborhood.

XU SIX: Even without introductions, she will come. Actually, she is my distant cousin. She, she, reckons I'm an honest guy, can rely on me rather than . . .

WU QI: Master Six, this is called being lucky with women . . .

XU SIX: Sergeant Wu, don't shame me. Have we ever caused trouble for anyone? Right under the Temple of Heaven we opened a small sock shop. They said they were building the airport. Down came our shop. You know that our Little Ni'er's mother had one hell of a temper. Well, she gave her life for that . . . (*tears well up in his eyes*).

WU QI: Master Six, I've caused you pain . . .

XU SIX: Look at me! My little girl's mother died not two months ago, and I'm off to the whore house to get myself a wife. . . . I'm no man. The child is too young . . . what can I do? . . . Okay, Elder Brother Liu, would you . . . (*exits*).

WU QI: Aiee! Every house has its own song of sorrow to sing. I still have contributions to collect . . . (*exits*).

LIU JIAXIANG (*walks over to the* chun *tree, grasping the Kitchen God by its neck and pointing the punk at the Kitchen God's nose*): What can I say? You've heard it all. The police commissioner has picked a mother up off the streets, so everyone else gets to make contributions. My stomach is full of bean curd dregs, and still I have to go work at the airport. (*The more he talks the angrier he becomes.*) I'll tell ya, that Guangdong candy I've given you, that's stolen from my own mouth. So when you get to Heaven, say good words for me. Don't let any nonsense slip out by accident! (*lights the paper image*). If you really have power, take this message to Fu Zuoyi: if he keeps fighting, he's a patsy! What's the use, telling you this? (*angrily stirs the ashes with the punk*). Go to Heaven! Piss off! (*turns in a huff and goes back into the courtyard*).

[Grandma Teng *wearing deep blue pants and a sky blue shirt appears at the north entrance of the lane. Her husband,* Teng Fengshan, *led a worker's strike in the Trolley Bus Factory and was executed at Yaotai, Beijing's execution ground. She was widowed in her thirties and is childless. Although poor, she is not without aspirations. She maintains herself by working as a maid.* Bi Wu, *who serves the flesh trade,*[19] *comes grinning from ear to ear carrying a neatly folded suit of shiny silk as he follows closely behind* Grandma Teng.]

BI WU (*begging*): . . . Madam, Madam, please try this on, try this on. The Thirty Six Salutes have been saluted,[20] now just slip into this . . .

GRANDMA TENG: . . . To be a maid, you don't have to dress me up like that. What is all this anyway? Tell me!

BI WU: . . . It's like this. We request you to come along, ah, to borrow you to help us . . . eh. You still don't understand? Come on, Grandma Teng, you're the sort who can take a hint. Haven't you seen Sergeant Wu handing out red slips all around? Commissioner Ding has his airplane ticket for tomorrow. Tonight he'll celebrate his mother's seventieth birthday, but he lacks the old lady . . .

GRANDMA TENG: You want me to be the family's mother?

BI WU: Otherwise, how can people say you are the lucky one? Is there a luckier job in all of Beiping? It's because you have such a good complexion. You're poor but carry a heroic countenance. Who doesn't know that Teng Fengshan, Master Teng, studied martial arts with "Li San the Swallow," killed the rich to help the poor. When Master Teng was alive . . . eh? Hey, hey, don't leave! (*chases after her*). You go enjoy a half a day of splendor. When it's over, we split it fifty-fifty—I get the clothes, you get the jewelry.

GRANDMA TENG (*throws the jewelry at* Bi Wu): Get out! This old lady will not stoop so low. I won't do such shameful things. Act as old Ding's mother? If I had such a wicked son, I'd strangle him as soon as he was born.

BI WU: Tsk. Here's a chance for face, and you turn it down? (*turning against her*). Don't you know what Bi Wu does?

GRANDMA TENG: You're just as bad as your father. Swindling and selling people . . .

BI WU (*cuts in*): I'll tell you! Old Bi Wu, was an official of the Seventh Rank in charge of the county board of punishment. He specialized in sending eunuchs to the Forbidden City. Are you going to act as old Ding's mother? You never had such damned luck (*bends over to pick up the costume jewelry*). Teng Fengshan, a stinking trolley driver, leads a worker's strike . . . and, to tell you the truth, Bi Wu with a single note sent him off to Yaotai.

GRANDMA TENG: Oh, what a nice guy! Finally it comes out it was you who did the dirty deed . . . (*lunges to grab* Bi Wu's *face*).

[*Just then* Third Son Water *comes out of the courtyard toting a water bucket.*]

BI WU: What? You want to fight me? (*grasps* Grandma Teng's *two wrists*). Ah! I haven't taken a good look at you. Twenty years ago, you must have been quite a looker (*suddenly he sees* Third Son Water; *he immediately lets* Grandma Teng *go*). Third Son Water? Third Master . . .

THIRD SON WATER (*puts down the water buckets*): You still recognize me?

BI WU (*forced to back up*): Who doesn't know you? You continue the family water delivery business for this lane . . .

THIRD SON WATER (*dignified*): I shall have to teach you a lesson.

BI WU: Don't! If you start scolding me, you may well continue for three days and three nights without repeating a single word. Your voice is as good as the radio's . . .

THIRD SON WATER: Present your buttocks then. Let me give it a couple of kicks.

BI WU (*cringing*): Third Master, please don't! You are the lineal successor of Master Teng. Your leg is just like an iron stick. Everyone knows that you are called "Golden Hook." I'm not worth even one kick from you . . .

THIRD SON WATER (*his voice like a thunderbolt*): Slap! Slap your own face!

[Bi Wu *begins to slap his own face.*]

THIRD SON WATER: Harder! Piss off!

BI WU (*not forgetting the jewelry on the ground before leaving*): Artificial, artificial jewelry is still useful (*exits*).

THIRD SON WATER: Shiniang,[21] it saddens my heart to see that you have to be a maid in one household after another. I lost my mother when I was little, and it's Master Teng who saved my life. Please let me take care of you . . .

[Liu Jiaxiang *comes out from the courtyard.*]

LIU JIAXIANG: It's you, Shiniang! How could you not come in when you pass by?

37

GRANDMA TENG: You have your own family and children and no idea of where to find food for your next meal . . .

LIU JIAXIANG: Master Teng died for us. No matter how hard the times are, we would have food for you, Grandma . . .

GRANDMA TENG: Don't say another word. . . . You've already lost your job. There's several mouths waiting for you to feed them. . . . Third Son, I'll live with you . . .

LIU JIAXIANG: Third Brother, then, then I put Shiniang in your hands. (*To* Grandma Teng) After these hard times are over, I'll send Er Niu to take you over . . .

[Third Son Water, *pulling his watercart, along with* Grandma Teng *and* Liu Jiaxiang, *exits from the south end of the lane.*]

[Elder Brother "Scarred Squint" *enters from the north, carrying candy figurines on his shoulder pole, leading* Er Niu *by the hand. On one side of the carrying pole there is an iron ladle with syrup inside it on the top of a stove. On the other side of the pole there is a square wooden box, covered by various figures of birds, animals, and household items, with a spinning dial in the middle of it. Children can play the spinning dial for one penny. Elder Brother "Scarred Squint" and* Er Niu *have just escaped a fight. Behind them the children still keep laughing at his physical defect: "Scarred Squint, went to the market, bought a radish that looks like a pear . . ."*][22]

ELDER BROTHER "SCARRED SQUINT" (*puts down his load and wipes the blood on the corner of his mouth*): Er Niu, you shouldn't stir up trouble again next time. That's the young owner of the "Zheng de he" store. His family runs a jewelry store.

ER NIU: I did nothing to provoke them. Elder Brother "Scarred Squint," they've hurt your mouth.

ELDER BROTHER "SCARRED SQUINT": It doesn't matter. You see (*wipes his mouth with the sleeve of his cotton padded jacket*), it's not bleeding anymore.

ER NIU: Elder Brother "Scarred Squint," when will you make a lantern for me? You still don't have time?

ELDER BROTHER "SCARRED SQUINT": Er Niu, you are a good girl. You see sometimes the spinning wheel stops where there is no figure, then I'll give that child a small piece of candy. But, if the needle stops at a figure of the phoenix or the lantern, I've got to use a lot of syrup to make that candy figurine. I would then earn no money that whole day. I would starve. Er Niu, you have your mother. I've no one to take care of me. Who feels for me? Er Niu feels for me . . .

ER NIU: Elder Brother "Scarred Squint," when will you have enough to eat?

ELDER BROTHER "SCARRED SQUINT": Listen, did you hear the bombing in the suburbs? (*Lowering his voice*) As soon as the Eighth Route Army enters the city, the poor will have enough to eat (*sitting behind his box, he weaves several iron wires into a cover*). The times need to change. People now steal and fight for food on the street. You see, Old Huang who sells sweet potatoes asked me to weave this iron cover for him. (*Suddenly remembers*) Oh, he gave me two roast sweet potatoes . . . (*takes out one from the under his seat*). Er Niu, here is one for you!

[Er Niu *takes it, smiling.*]

ELDER BROTHER "SCARRED SQUINT": Is it sweet? Er Niu, you're a smart girl. Why don't you ask your mother to send you to school?

ER NIU: If I wanted to go to school, my parents would first have to give the principal a golden ring and delicacies . . .

ELDER BROTHER "SCARRED SQUINT": Oh, you sure can't afford that!

[Fortune-teller Yang *returns again. He is singing that "Song of Great Peace" while walking. He stops in front of* Er Niu.]

FORTUNE-TELLER YANG (*gulps when his eyes fix on* Er Niu's *sweet potato*): What are you eating, Er Niu? (*grinds his teeth, hacks, and spits on* Er Niu's *sweet potato*).

ER NIU: What are you doing? You pay for it! Pay for it! (*throws the potato away, crying*).

[Fortune-teller Yang *picks up the sweet potato, brushes and dusts it off, and quickly pops it into his mouth.*]

ELDER BROTHER "SCARRED SQUINT": You're a grown man! Stealing food from a kid . . .

FORTUNE-TELLER YANG (*rolls his eyes*): Don't you know I'm shameless . . .

ELDER BROTHER "SCARRED SQUINT" (*hands his own sweet potato to* Er Niu): Er Niu, please stop crying (*seeing that Er Niu keeps crying, takes out a few cigarette cases folded in the shape of triangles from his pocket*). Er Niu, these are for you. Triangles! They are made from "Camel," "Red Soldier," and "Old Sword" packs . . . (*picks up his candy figurines and leads* Er Niu *into the courtyard*).

[Little Ring, *who sells fake medicines, walks in with a vinegar pot hid under his cotton padded jacket and a bunch of chopsticks in the sleeves. His jacket is dirty and covered with grease spots. But his face is beaming with satisfaction. Conspicuously, he also has an old shabby American jacket over his arm. Behind him a waiter from Unity Restaurant follows, at a proper distance.*]

LITTLE RING: Hello! Fortune-teller Yang.

FORTUNE-TELLER YANG: Oh, it's you, Little Ring.

LITTLE RING: Guess where I've been to today? The Unity Restaurant. Malian pork, pork with tofu, and three tasty dumplings . . . great! The food was just great! I haven't had such good food for a long, long time.

FORTUNE-TELLER YANG: You? Look at your shabby clothes.

LITTLE RING: I borrowed this jacket! (*shakes the jacket*). An American jacket. Can't you see? These days you have to look sharp. Selling those fake medicines, I couldn't even afford a drink of bean juice. (*takes out the vinegar pot from his jacket*). Unity, the oldest and best restaurant. Take a look, even the vinegar pot is posh, porcelain from Jingde zhen.[23]

WAITER (*walks close by*): Will you let me follow you to where you get the money?

LITTLE RING: The Eighth Route Army is going to enter the city soon. Have you heard that? The dynasty is going to change. Shouldn't each person have some fun? (*patting his chest*). I am a worthy customer. Don't be such a money grub.

WAITER: What kind of worthy customer are you? After eating, you took off without paying. You even swiped our vinegar pot and a bunch of chopsticks.

LITTLE RING (*pats the waiter's shoulder*): How about this: today, anyway, you treat me; tomorrow, I treat you! We two go to the Harvest Garden Restaurant tomorrow. Otherwise, the Smooth Restaurant, instant-boiled mutton. You choose the place. Fine, are you still worried about the money? (*from his jacket, he takes out a small box covered by glass and tied with a red ribbon*). You take this box of ginseng . . .

WAITER (*grasps the box and throws it on the ground without taking a look inside*): Ginseng? Don't fool with me! Roots and stems of weeds (*wrestles the vinegar pot from* Little Ring). Anyway, it's a bad day for our owner (*turns and leaves*).

FORTUNE-TELLER YANG (*kicks the box lightly*): Well, I've learned one more trick (*exits*).

[Little Ring *bends over to pick up his "ginseng."* Liu Jiaxiang *and* Auntie Liu *lead* Little Sturdy *in from the south entrance of the lane.* Wu Qi *totes a dozen socks on his shoulder as he enters from the north end.*]

WU QI: Buy a pair of socks to wear? (*Seeing that it's* Liu Jiaxiang) Oh! It's Brother Liu? (*pulls back his hand*).

LIU JIAXIANG: So, you sell socks as well as hand out contribution slips?

WU QI: Just this once. If I do it again, I won't be a man! Some soldiers robbed the yarn shop. I was able to pick up a dozen socks. If I am lying to you, then I'm a bastard. . . . (*To* Auntie Liu) Have you finished that business for your child?

AUNTIE LIU: I think the old Taoist priest was so hungry he lost his mind. He just patted Little Sturdy on the head and pronounced his Buddhist name as Seng Bao[24] and sent us home. Who is he kidding?

LITTLE RING (*seeing* Little Sturdy, *narrows his eyes and goes over to him saying pretentiously*): Ah, Little Sturdy has grown so big! (*looks cunningly at* Wu Qi).

WU QI (*wants to escape*): All right, Brother Liu, go about your business . . .

LITTLE RING (*grabbing* Wu Qi's *arm*): Master Qi, don't go! (*With a threatening laugh*) Master Qi, you've got some dander! You play both sides of the fence. . . . When you put Little Sturdy at the entrance of the lane, he was just three or four years old, eh?

WU QI (*frightened*): You, what are you getting at?

LITTLE RING: You really are the well-fed man who fails to understand the hungry. Don't you think you should buy me off? (*uses his eyes to take aim at* Auntie Liu).

AUNTIE LIU: Little Ring! If you mean to sell us out, then do your stuff. I don't have a cent. You creep, you spread shit every chance you get. If the King of Hell hadn't been napping, you would never have put on human skin. Little Sturdy, let's go (*leads* Little Sturdy *into the courtyard*).

LITTLE RING: We've all been living on the street for a long time. Anyway, I should get something out of it, too.

WU QI: How about this—here have a couple pairs of socks. Is this enough? (*gives* Little Ring *the socks*). What on earth is this all about . . . ? (*exits*).

LITTLE RING (*takes the sock*): Elder Brother Liu, it's your turn now. How about you cook me some noodles! Otherwise, find me some peanuts . . .

LIU JIAXIANG (*walks into the courtyard*): Me? I may have some rat poison in my house.

LITTLE RING (*follows him*): Don't say that (*enters the courtyard*). How can you . . . (*exits*).

[*The back door of the Wei Family opens with a squeak. Ma Deqing, an old servant, walks out with a lantern.*]

MA DEQING (*holding the lantern to light the threshold*): Third Young Master, step over the threshold.

[*Third Young Master of the Wei Family,* Qishi'er, *nicely dressed and looking just like a son of a wealthy family, walks out from the back door.*]

QISHI'ER (*his eyes are full of fear*): Old Ma, where are you taking me?

MA DEQING: I am taking you to your old grand-aunt's house.

QISHI'ER (*his voice quivers*): You're fooling with me! You are taking me to the Tangen'er[25] . . . (*suddenly, with a plop, he kneels down*).

MA DEQING: What are you doing? What the hell is this about: how could the master kneel in front of me, a servant?

QISHI'ER: I heard everything! Why do they want to kill me?

[Ma Deqing *immediately blows out the lantern and hurriedly closes the back door of the Wei Family.*]

QISHI'ER: In front of outsiders, I was treated as a Third Young Master. But in the Wei Family, I am a lowly lackey, a slave. . . . You are the only one who is kind to me.

MA DEQING: Stand up! You stand up! Listen to me, I'll tell you the whole truth.

[Qishi'er *stands up.*]

MA DEQING: Do you still remember that the Wei Family had a banquet on the day they bought you? Baldy Wei told the guests at the banquet that you were his youngest son. He had just brought you home from Suzhou. Among the guests there was a person who speaks with a Tianjin accent . . .

QISHI'ER (*nods his head continuously*): Is that the one who has two big eyeballs?

MA DEQING: Yes, that's him. That person is the chief manager of a life insurance company. Baldy Wei bought life insurance for you from that company. Your father, Baldy Wei, is such a son of a bitch! He is going to leave by air the day after tomorrow. So tonight he asked me to take you to the Tangan'er (*takes out a paper bag from his pocket*) and make you eat this poisoned cake. After you die, they'll go to that life insurance company to collect the money. Do you understand now?

[Qishi'er *kneels down again.*]

MA DEQING: Qishi'er, stand up. Don't make me anxious (*takes out a roll of money from his pocket with a trembling hand*). Take the money with you. Go! Hurry up!

QISHI'ER: And you?

MA DEQING: Don't worry about me! I have places to go (*stares at Qish'er with deep love*). I've already got one foot in the grave. Got no family or kids. If your future is good, remember to come back to see me sometimes . . .

QISHI'ER (*all of a sudden*): Father.

MA DEQING: Go! Hurry up!

[*They exit from different directions. After a while, the mistress of the Shi Family,* Auntie Shi, *walks out and looks around.*]

AUNTIE SHI (*mutters with a low voice*): Black boy, white boy, sit on the bed and eat dumplings (*clears her voice*). Black boy, white boy . . .

[Shopkeeper Shi, *who runs a small business, comes out from the courtyard.*]

SHOPKEEPER SHI (*catches* Auntie Shi *in a few steps*): It's too soon to pray for a son. People do this on New Year's Eve! You've only added to our unhappiness on this holiday.

AUNTIE SHI: Don't you see I am practicing? You're annoying!

SHOPKEEPER SHI: Day in and day out, if I am not going off to build the airport, then it's digging trenches. My heart is in my throat all day long. Have children? These days even hens stop laying eggs . . .

AUNTIE SHI: Fate! The ancestors of the Shi Family must have done something bad. Otherwise, how can the Shi Family be without offspring . . .

[*Just then the streetlights turn off.*]

SHOPKEEPER SHI: All right, the fucking electricity is down again. All you do is complain. Don't you know that I've much more trouble than you do? We used to run a rice store. But now we are going to be out of rice ourselves.

AUNTIE SHI: Are you blaming me?! Just when I had made dough rise for baking, several stinky soldiers came in and cooked and ate all of it.

SHOPKEEPER SHI: Billeting soldiers in our houses. . . . How I wish I could bury them all alive!

[*Two soldiers of the KMT army walk out with a large basin that is used for leavening dough.*]

SOLDIER A: Shopkeeper Shi! We are going to be transferred. You are good to our brothers. We really don't want to leave your house. But you know we are soldiers who have no choice. (*Holding the basin up*) We'll take this basin with us as a memento.

SHOPKEEPER SHI (*pretending to be happy*): See you tomorrow, officers! (*Seeing the soldiers already gone, he gnashes his teeth.*) See you tomorrow? Tomorrow the Eighth Route Army enters the city and will kill you all! (*Suddenly realizes*) How could they be transferred again? (*To* Auntie Shi) Is Little Liben at home?

AUNTIE SHI: Yes, he is. (*Yelling toward the courtyard*) Little Liben! Little Liben!

[Little Liben *is the favorite shop assistant to the Shi Family. He runs out.*]

LITTLE LIBEN: Auntie Shi, are you calling me?

SHOPKEEPER SHI: Little Liben, it looks like the Eighth Route Army isn't going to enter the city yet. We must keep some rice for ourselves! You go to the store to take care of business there. Don't sell that last bag of rice, even if customers are willing to pay with a wagon full of gold. Remember that. Go! Hurry up!

[Chen Jiuling, *the cook for the KMT army, wearing a filthy uniform, comes from the south entrance.*]

CHEN JIULING (*calling loudly*): Master Shi! Auntie Shi!

SHOPKEEPER SHI: Is that you, Little Jiu? Why do you still wear this "tiger skin"?

CHEN JIULING: I was forced to join the KMT army. (*Lowering his voice*) Master Shi, did you know that Deng Baoshan[26] and Zhang Dongsun left the city from the West Gate?

SHOPKEEPER SHI: Zhang Dongsun?

CHEN JIULING: He's the professor from Yanjing University! Also, a representative of General Fu Zuoyi. (*Hearing the muffled sounds of bombing in the distance*) They're bombing again. Little Liben, the head of our bureau asked me to collect the receipt for the rice we bought last year.

LITTLE LIBEN (*hands him the receipt*): Brother Chen, the receipt was written according to the old rule: 150 lbs. bag was put down as 180 lbs., and 10 dollars a bag was recorded as 12 dollars a bag ...

SHOPKEEPER SHI: Little Liben, you can add more. So Little Jiu can get a bit, too.

CHEN JIULING: It won't work!

SHOPKEEPER SHI: The Eighth Route Army is coming into the city soon.

CHEN JIULING: The Eighth Route Army forbids accepting bribes or extorting ...

SHOPKEEPER SHI: You are so muddle-headed! Just look at the receipt for your bureau head.

CHEN JIULING: That's natural! He is the head of the bureau. Who doesn't want to eat good food or drink nice wine? Isn't that right, Auntie Shi?

AUNTIE SHI: Why can he take bribes and you can't? Ask him.

CHEN JIULING: Auntie Shi, you're truly thinking for me. But am I tired of living? If I did that, they would send me to the military court in a flash. It would be no joke.

[*They enter the courtyard, except* Little Liben, *who exits from the north end.*]

[*Former prostitute* Spring Happiness, *following* Xu Six, *enters from the south end. When they reach the old big* chun *tree,* Spring Happiness *stops, hesitating.*]

XU SIX (*can't help saying*): There's still time for you to change your mind. . . . I'm very poor. I've nothing in my house.

SPRING HAPPINESS (*sincerely*): Poor, I'm not afraid of being poor. I'm finally a human again since I left that brothel. . . . But you must talk to your old neighbors. Nobody can look down on me! If they do, I swear there is nothing I won't do!

XU SIX: You don't need to worry about it. Except for the Liu Family, no one in the neighborhood knows about your past. From now on I'll do whatever you want, except one thing: You must be kind to Little Ni'er ...

SPRING HAPPINESS: Do you want me to swear? I lost my mother, too, when I was little. I'm only twenty-four. I can give you a son. How great it will be: one son and one daughter.

[Little Ring *walks out the courtyard while picking his teeth with a matchstick.*]

LITTLE RING: Xu Six? Master Six . . . this is . . . (*walks closely to* Spring Happiness *and recognizes her*). Wow! Isn't this Spring Happiness? (*claps his thigh and raises his voice*). Are you going to marry Xu Six? Hey! This is funny . . . Master Xu, tomorrow, from tomorrow, I'll never be able to touch Spring Happiness again . . .

XU SIX (*doesn't know how to stop* Little Ring): Little Ring! Little Ring!

[*All the neighbors pour out after they hear the news.*]

LITTLE RING (*so excited that he seems to lose control of himself*): Master Xu, you are a good judge of women! Spring Happiness, Spring Happiness is truly sexy! (*narrowing his eyes and shaking his head, profuse in praise*). Yum! Yum!

LIU JIAXIANG: Little Ring! Are you human?

[Auntie Liu *and* Auntie Shi *rush to soothe* Spring Happiness.]

AUNTIE LIU: Xu Six! How can you take such needling? Don't you have a hand? Slap him! Slap the bastard!

LITTLE RING (*giggles and puts his face close to* Spring Happiness): Right. Sister, slap me. Little Ring won't let you down. If you use your little hand to pat my face, I promise you I won't wash my face for six months . . .

[Spring Happiness *cries and runs into the courtyard.*]

XU SIX (*stretches his hand and moves close to* Little Ring. *He tries hard but finally slaps himself instead*): Xu Six, where is your backbone? The others have already sat on your shoulder and shit on you, still you dare not fight back? (*weeps*).

[*The neighbors pull* Xu Six *into the courtyard.*]

LITTLE RING: Don't be angry with me. Master Six, don't be angry with me (*giggles and exits*).

[Little Sturdy *stands in front of the gate timidly and bites his fingers.* Bi Wu *enters from the north with candied haws[27] on a stick in his hand.*]

BI WU: Come here! Little Sturdy, come here! Here have candied haws . . . (*exits*).

[Bi Wu's *curses between his teeth can be heard: "Little bastard! You, come here." Just at this moment* Third Son Water *comes over and hears* Little Sturdy's *cries.*]

THIRD SON WATER (*screams*): Auntie Liu! Auntie Liu! Little Sturdy has been kidnapped!

[*People, except* Auntie Shi *and* Spring Happiness, *all pour out into the courtyard.*]

PEOPLE (*cry out anxiously*): Little Sturdy!

[*As the people go to catch the kidnapper, suddenly they hear, "Glug, glug, glug," from the left side.*]

THIRD SON WATER (*stops*): Who pulled out the plug! Fuck him whoever pulled the plug out of my watercart! Little Ring, you stop (*chases and exits*).

[Auntie Shi *runs out the courtyard in a flurry.*]

AUNTIE SHI: Xu Six! Xu Six! Spring Happiness has drunk arsenic. Spring Happiness has drunk arsenic.

[Spring Happiness *rushes out with disheveled hair.*]

SPRING HAPPINESS (*grasps* Xu Six's *arm*): I can't bear to suffer anymore. I've drunk arsenic. I want to live, but this world won't let me live . . .

XU SIX (*stamps his feet*): You can't drink poison. You shouldn't drink poison.

[People *pull* Spring Happiness *into the courtyard to make her throw up. . . . The empty space calms down suddenly. . . . The buzzing of airplanes and the booming of the Eighth Route Army's great guns return from the distance. Sporadic and scattered sounds of firecrackers and a desolate voice selling candy melon rise.*

Suddenly the street lights turn on. Along with his clear and melodi-

ous announcement, Little Liben, *strong and vigorous, flashes into Small Well Lane. Little Liben's shouts crack like a clap of spring thunder above Beiping.*]

LITTLE LIBEN: Read the news! Read the news! Read *Beiping Daily, North China Daily!* Read General Fu Zuoyi's announcement: The peaceful liberation of Beiping has been signed. An agreement reached. Read the news! Read the news!

[*The old neighbors of Small Well Lane pour onto the street together. Little Liben, with newspapers on his shoulder and the red armband of "Worker Guards"*[28] *on his arm, softly smiles at his old neighbors.*]

SHOPKEEPER SHI (*calls out in a happy astonishment*): Little Liben, it's you! You're a . . .

[*Someone's rooster chooses this moment to crow. The first crow brings a chorus of crowing throughout the city.*]

(CURTAIN)

Discussing how to make steel in 1958 (from the stage production).

ACT TWO

TIME Late summer 1958. Sunset. This is the year of the "Great Leap Forward." Everyone in Small Well Lane and China is attempting to make a great leap for the nation's economy.[29] It is a dreamlike time. Everyone is mesmerized by the dream of achieving true communism in China tomorrow . . .

PLACE Compound No. 7, Small Well Lane.

SCENE This is a very common compound household.[30] The front of the compound includes two rooms facing east. One room is occupied by Liu Jiaxiang and his family. The Chen Jiuling couple and their son, Big Ox, live next door. The south side of the compound has only one and a half rooms. Xu Six's family lives in one. The other half-room is now used to store Elder Brother "Scarred Squint"'s remaining household items. The Shi Family owns the compound. They live in the north side and have more rooms than the other families. A small passageway runs to the inner courtyard. In the inner courtyard there is nothing but a house with two small rooms. One is the Shi Family's storage room. The other is left for Little Liben's wife, who is called Little Mrs.

In the main courtyard, on the north wall of Lius' house, a water tap has just been installed. The whole compound looks clean, pretty, and relaxed.

In the distance a middle school has recently been built. A slogan is written on the wall of the red brick building: "Education Serves the Political Needs of the Proletariat!" Part of the slogan is covered by the stage curtain.

[CURTAIN RISES *with choral singing, "Chairman Mao Comes to Our Village," being practiced in the school. The clear and melodious voices of children waft into the courtyard. The old neighbors are having a neighborhood meeting.* Liu Jiaxiang, Auntie Liu, Shopkeeper Shi, Xu Six, *and two new members are scattered around the courtyard on their stools. The shy woman who is stitching the sole of a cloth shoe is* Auntie Jiu, Chen Jiuling's *wife. Another young woman with a smile on her lips and a calculating mind is surnamed Zhou, but the neighbors call her* Little Mrs. *She is the wife of* Little Liben. *A politically ambitious woman, she is now a fearsome rising "new star" in the old neighborhood.*

In these years it was popular to sing a revolutionary song before a meeting. The grown Er Niu *stands on the steps in front of the neighbors and teaches them a song, "Socialism Is Good!"*]

ER NIU (*shakes the song sheet in her hand*): Uncle Shi: Don't be impatient. When you sang, you used the correct words, and the correct tune, but you didn't put them together. The last line of the song should be sung this way (*sings*):

   The people throughout the country join together
   To launch a new wave of Socialist Production, of
      Socialist Production.

SHOPKEEPER SHI: Girl, my throat is like a chimney. It can't twist round all that. This throat will work for the marketplace (*yelling*): "Hey, don't cut in the line!" Er Niu, you . . .

ER NIU: You called me Er Niu again! It has been nine years since liberation—you still call us Er Niu and Missy Liu . . .

SHOPKEEPER SHI: Guiying. Liu Guiying. Next time Uncle Shi forgets again, you can call me by my nickname, Little Crooked.

AUNTIE LIU (*stands up*): Guiying, you can stop teaching the song now. Anyway, the leadership says that everybody must know how to sing this song before October 1.[31] The neighborhood committee held a meeting this afternoon. You may have already heard what happened in the meeting. (*Takes out a small piece of white cloth from her pocket*) We, No. 7 Compound, got a white flag for our steelmaking.[32] See here (*points to* Little Mrs., *who sits next to her*), the Rectification Leadership Small Group sent her to help us. She is educated and in charge of the woolen knitwear street factory. Her husband joined the Volunteer Army to fight in Korea.³³ (*To* Little Mrs.) Little Zhou, please stand up and let everybody get to know you.

[Little Mrs. *stands up and smiles to everybody. She flaunts a "fountain pen" on the front of her Chinese blouse.*]³⁴

AUNTIE LIU: We have many people living in this compound. It's difficult to have everyone come. Auntie Jiu, where is Little Jiu?

AUNTIE JIU: He went to work. He is busy building the "Ten Great Constructions" and also the backyard steel furnaces.³⁵

AUNTIE LIU: And Auntie Shi? Where is Auntie Shi?

AUNTIE JIU: Yesterday she asked me to give her a skein of colored thread. She may have gone to the Goddess Temple to pray for a child.

[*Suddenly red lights appear in the distant sky. Immediately a deafening sound of gongs and drums pours into the lane. People run out the street gate one after another.*]

LIU JIAXIANG: Must be Large Well Lane! Large Well Lane has succeeded in steelmaking!

LITTLE MRS.: Large Well Lane has succeeded now; how about Small Well Lane? Old neighbors, we of No. 7 Compound shouldn't be holding Small Well Lane back. We must come up with some good ideas right away . . .

LIU JIAXIANG: This is disgraceful (*in his anxiety he suddenly sees the iron knockers on the gate*). Hey! How could I forget them? (*Walks over and attempts to take them off*).

SHOPKEEPER SHI: How many ounces of iron can the knockers give? Auntie Liu, we still need to find abandoned cannons . . .

PEOPLE: Cannons? Where can you find abandoned cannons?

AUNTIE LIU: Let me tell you. Yesterday Elder Brother Shi mentioned that our next-door neighbor's house used to be the location of a fort in the Qing Dynasty. Maybe some abandoned cannons are buried there under the house. But, we'll have to tear down the house first to find out whether or not there are cannons . . .

[*Sounds of voices yelling and ladders being hoisted to the roof float in from next door. Then sounds of bricks and tiles falling on the ground.*]

SHOPKEEPER SHI: Listen, Listen! No. 5 Compound has started to tear down the house. As for the fort, I heard that from the others, too. These old rooms in the south end of compound belong to me. To make a Great Leap Forward in the economy, I'm willing to cut flesh from my own body.[36] If I hesitate, I'm not a man of loyalty! (*feels embarrassed and spreads his hands with a shrug*). But you all know that Xu Six and his family live in one room, and the other half-room is full of Elder Brother "Scarred Squint"'s stuff . . .

LIU JIAXIANG: Elder Brother Shi, don't hesitate. The government needs our support now. Let's be fair. Have we ever seen such a good government before?! Do you remember the movements against the three evils and the five evils? Do you remember the Movement to Suppress Counterrevolutionaries?[37] Bi Wu was executed in that movement. The Public Security Bureau helped us find Little Sturdy through the newspapers . . .

XU SIX: This government has been great to us. But, as for pulling down the house, we should think about it carefully. You can't get fruit from a tree when there isn't any, no matter how hard you hit it.

AUNTIE JIU: Auntie Liu, why don't you first go to the House Property Bureau and check the records. If a sewer pipe had been installed under the house, I don't think there will still be abandoned cannons there. But if there is no sewer pipe, maybe . . .

[*The noise of pulling down the house next door increases. Someone is crying: "Look out! Look out! One, two, three, pull! Pull. . . ."* Auntie Shi, *beaming with satisfaction, runs in.*]

AUNTIE SHI: Oh, having a meeting?

AUNTIE LIU: Did you go to the Goddess Temple again?

AUNTIE SHI: The Goddess Temple was pulled down long ago. Wu Qi told me that a forty-eight-year-old woman in Oil Basket Lane just gave birth to a son, an eight and a half pound boy! I went to take a look. . . . I'm thirty-nine this year—I still have nine years to keep hoping . . .

[*The door of* Xu Six's *house opens with a loud bang. But nobody comes out.*]

LITTLE MRS. (*lowering voice to ask Auntie Liu*): Who is inside?

AUNTIE LIU: Spring Happiness. In the Rectification Movement she and Auntie Shi fought. They haven't talked to each other since.

[*Inside* Xu Six's *house* Spring Happiness *turns on the radio. Singing pours out:* "Each year we like to sing songs, / but there is no year we've sung as many as this year . . ."]

AUNTIE SHI (*she directs her words to* Xu Six's *house with a darkened face*): Tell me if you are looking for trouble! Don't you try to lay like a dead weight on others' heads . . .

SHOPKEEPER SHI: Can't you shut your mouth?

AUNTIE SHI: Is this a neighborhood or brothel? Small Well Lane is too small for her to stay.

XU SIX (*has to stand up and walk over to his house*): Would you please turn down the radio? We are discussing things now . . .

[*Instead, the radio goes up. Just then* Xu Six's *daughter,* Little Ni'er, *comes in with a red scarf*[38] *on her neck and several copies of the* Beijing Evening News *in her hand.*]

LITTLE NI'ER: Auntie Liu, Large Well Lane succeeded in steelmaking! The district head went there with big red flowers . . . (*the newspapers fall down from her hands as she talks excitedly*). Oh, I was so caught up in watching the steelmaking that I forgot to sell newspapers. My mom will beat me again . . . (*wants to cry*).

SHOPKEEPER SHI: Don't cry, Little Ni'er. Evening newspapers are easy to sell. You sell all of them to Uncle Shi! (*snatches the newspapers and then from his pocket takes out a handful of pennies and puts them into* Little Ni'er's *hands*). Take them. Two cents, four cents, six cents . . .

[Spring Happiness *blows out the door like a gust of wind and is in front of people in no time. Her finger points to* Little Ni'er's *nose.*]

SPRING HAPPINESS (*sternly*): Give the money back! Give the money back! Do you hear me?

[Little Ni'er *puts back the money into* Shopkeeper Shi's *hand without hesitation.*]

SHOPKEEPER SHI (*smiles bitterly*): Why you are so angry with us . . . ?

SPRING HAPPINESS: You make a fool of yourself! (*slaps* Little Ni'er *while dragging her*). Going around the world, having a grand old time? You went to the Peach of Immortality Palace. You went to the Goddess Temple. No matter where you've been to, you're still a parasite. A hen can lay eggs. We feed you for what? . . .

[Auntie Shi *jumps up but is pushed down by* Auntie Liu.]

AUNTIE LIU: Don't stir up more trouble.

LIU JIAXIANG: Little Ni'er's mother, now this is your fault. Little Ni'er went to join the Great Leap Forward. But you scold her and hit her. You've disturbed the peace of the whole neighborhood . . .

AUNTIE SHI (*finding that people are not on* Spring Happiness's *side, brushes away* Auntie Liu's *hand and walks up to* Spring Happiness): Just who were you bad-mouthing?

SPRING HAPPINESS: Who am I bad-mouthing? You have no place to speak.

AUNTIE SHI: Why should I have no place to speak here? Explain yourself.

SPRING HAPPINESS: Where does salt get its saltiness? Vinegar its sourness? You are using others to bully me!

LITTLE MRS. (*clearing her throat*): The problem in Compound No. 7 isn't a matter of just one or two days. The Rectification Movement not only hasn't brought unity but, instead, has added new problems. One problematic compound will hold Small Well Lane back, and a troubled Small Well Lane will become a drag on the district's Great Leap Forward. Our meeting today is in fact a supplementary class for solving these problems. Lay your dispute on the table . . .

SPRING HAPPINESS: In last spring's rectification and self-education meetings I merely said that Auntie Shi (*points to the swallow's nest under the eaves*), that you shouldn't oppose the movement to shoo away sparrows just because of this swallow's nest . . .[39]

AUNTIE SHI: Who is against shooing away the sparrows? They're living creatures, too. If the old swallow is shooed away and doesn't dare to come feed young swallows, they would all starve to death.

SPRING HAPPINESS: So just for that you cursed me as childless. Who knows who'll be childless in the end! You know I was angry. But you have done something that will break your family line. What did you say to our Little Ni'er? Tell everybody here what you said.

AUNTIE SHI (*knows that she is in the wrong but won't accept fault*): Little Ni'er is a big girl now. She knew everything, even if I hadn't told her.

SPRING HAPPINESS: She knows? That's because you told her. (*Sadly*) I've married Xu Six for nine years. Yes, I didn't give him a child. But, this isn't my fault. As for you two, who doesn't know your calculation? You think I don't know the reason you suggested we tear down this house? These days people say those who own more than fifteen rooms should hand them over to the public. And, even without these one and a half rooms, you already own fifteen rooms. Didn't you just say that you wouldn't cry even if a piece of your flesh was cut off? I've heard more than you wanted to say! (*slaps* Little Ni'er *one more time*). Go inside! From now on I'll beat you every day!

[Little Cao, *now a policeman, enters the courtyard.*]

LITTLE MRS.: Today's dispute hasn't been settled; we'll continue to discuss it.

AUNTIE LIU: Little Ni'er, go wash your face first. In all fairness Auntie Shi shouldn't sow dissension among family members. But, Spring Happiness, you've mistreated Little Ni'er too long.

[Spring Happiness, Xu Six, *and* Little Ni'er *go into their house.*]

SHOPKEEPER SHI: Comrade Cao, please come, you know best who is right and who is wrong . . .

LITTLE CAO: Uncle Shi. Don't be worried. The state isn't going to take your house away but will manage it on your behalf. Don't you understand? Now, old neighbors, the third group of the Volunteer Army have returned from Korea. (*To* Little Mrs.) You are assigned to live in the house in the inner courtyard. I've arranged it with Uncle Shi. The room in Compound No. 3 is too small. Your husband is a "most honorable man."[40] Uncle Shi, do you agree with me?

SHOPKEEPER SHI: Oh, I agree with you. Life in Korea is definitely hard, hanging heads on their waistbands and eating parched flour with snow. They are the nation's heroes and honorable servants. (*To* Auntie Shi) Let's go clean that room . . . (*the* Shis *enter the inner courtyard*).

LITTLE MRS.: I'll go take a look at the house (*follows the* Shis *into the inner courtyard*).

ER NIU: Comrade Cao, is Elder Brother "Scarred Squint" among the discharged soldiers?

LITTLE CAO: We don't know his proper name; it's a bit difficult to find him.

AUNTIE LIU: We heard from him in the first two years of the war. But since then . . . I've got a knot in my heart.

[Ma Deqing, *the former servant of the Wei Family, enters.*]

MA DEQING (*shouts as he enters*): You're here! I've been looking for you all over the place. Little Cao, you have a phone call. From the police office.

LITTLE CAO: Uncle Ma, you've been working so well lately. I've received dozens of letters from the old neighbors praising you. You not only did a good job at the public telephone station but also helped to clean the street. Look, look at Small Well Lane—the street always shines like a mirror.

MA DEQING (*blushes*): Please don't say that. Who doesn't want to put in a bit more effort to make a Great Leap Forward?

LITTLE CAO: I'm off! My old neighbors, do your best. Have you heard that another new "satellite"[41] rises in Hunan province? 15,000 lbs. of grain was grown in one *mu*.[42] It's said that children can play on top of the grain stalks and won't fall in. Auntie Liu, ask each family to hand in the rats' tails.[43] The leader is going to count them before judging which family is number one in wiping out rats. As for scrap iron and copper, try to collect more. . . . All right, I am off to answer the phone (*exits*).

MA DEQING (*walks close to* Liu Jiaxiang): Brother Liu, I just received a letter from my son. He'll be home in a few days. If he returns, he'll come to Compound No. 7 to look for me. Please let everyone know that they should tell him to find me at the street factory.

LIU JIAXIANG: Brother Ma, your son has really won honor for you! During that turmoil and chaos, he not only found a way to escape from Beijing but also joined the Eighth Route Army and became a reporter.

AUNTIE LIU: We haven't heard from him for more than six months. You must have been worried; we are all sixes and sevens about it. You know that not long ago many educated people seemed to have gotten into trouble . . .[44]

MA DEQING: There are no outsiders here. Tell you the truth: life totally changed after I adopted this son. I'm not afraid of your looking down on me. My uncle served at the palace in the late Qing Dynasty. He was a eunuch. I was his adopted son. As for me, I worked as a servant for the Wei Family most of my life. I had no kids. Who would have thought that, just before liberation, I would adopt such a wonderful son who earns me such dignity? I must say, my heart is full of gusto! I feel like I am flying everyday. Beautiful! (*Lowering his voice*) Brother Shi is here. (*Raising his voice*) Okay, see you again (*exits*).

[*The* Shis, *carrying a jumble of things, emerge from the inner courtyard with* Little Mrs. . . .]

SHOPKEEPER SHI (*brushes the dust off his clothes*): That house is ready for you to move in.

LITTLE MRS.: Uncle Shi, thank you for taking so much trouble. (*To everybody*) Anyway, in this rectification study we should also offer critical opinions to the leaders. (*Sounding the others out*) I heard that Little Cao approved 30 lbs. of rice coupons for a temporary resident in Compound No. 3.[45] Furthermore, I feel Little Cao isn't easy to approach. But to say he is bureaucratic might be going too far . . .

AUNTIE LIU: That's because you haven't known him long enough. Little Cao is a very honest and solid young man!

LITTLE MRS. (*quickly changes her tone*): That's right. We agree about him. But the higher level leaders asked us to offer critical opinions. What's to be done? What I just said is from someone's muddled report. Anyway, Auntie Liu, you still take the lead in the neighborhood committee. I'll be your helper. All right, I've a room now; I'm going to move in (*exits*).

[*Everyone begins to return their own home. Chen Jiuling, wearing a construction worker's uniform, enters the courtyard with a hat in his hand and full of vigor.*]

CHEN JIULING (*cries out as soon as he enters*): Big Ox's mother! Big Ox's mother! Uncle Shi! Auntie Shi!

[Shopkeeper Shi, *the* Lius, *and* Chen Jiuling's *wife stop.*]

AUNTIE JIU: What are you up to now? (*To* Auntie Liu) You see. He's a grown man but doesn't take anything seriously.

CHEN JIULING: I had a great meeting today! A great meeting. I need a couple of drinks!

SHOPKEEPER SHI: What meeting?

CHEN JIULING: The meeting "to open your heart to your leaders" (*gesturing as he speaks*). There are more than two thousand workers in my company. This one guy had a historical problem; another guy is an active counterrevolutionary.... Confess yourself if you have done anything that makes you feel you let the government down. This is called opening your heart to your leaders (*covers half of his mouth*). To tell you the truth, most people in my company are the dregs of society. After one person finished confessing his own guilt, the leader walked over to pat him on the shoulders, and the manager shook his hand and encouraged him. I was jealous but had nothing to confess. (*Enviously*) The leader pats your shoulders. This is no joke! I told myself: Chen Jiuling, this is the time to show your dedication. Nothing to confess? Well, make something up! Come on!

SHOPKEEPER SHI: Did you really make up confession?

CHEN JIULING: Sure! I'm not lying. I got on the stage and confessed. I made the whole confession up! True or false doesn't matter, as long as it fits. I told them I provided the blacklist that got the five workers arrested in the Trolley Bus Factory strike in 1947 . . .

LIU JIAXIANG: Did you provide the blacklist?

CHEN JIULING: No, of course not. The whole confession was made up (*keeps talking*). As soon as I, Chen Jiuling, confessed, I earned unanimous applause. The leader came over and patted my shoulders. I'm an advanced element. This meeting was wonderful!

AUNTIE JIU: How can you pour shit on your own head? The cops will come and get you. How can you be so stupid! (*so upset she slaps her thighs*).

LIU JIAXIANG: Tomorrow, get up early and rush directly to your factory. Tell the truth. Tell your leaders that you took the wrong medicine yesterday and made the whole confession up . . .

CHEN JIULING: It can't be so serious? Can it be so serious? Anyway, first I need a nap.

[Chen *enters his house, and* Auntie Jiu *follows him.* Grandma Teng *walks in with a walking stick.*]

GRANDMA TENG: Fengzhen! Fengzhen! (*moves close to* Auntie Liu *and lowers her voice*). Is it true that Compound No. 7 got a white flag? (*takes out a small cloth bag from her blouse*). I've got a small bronze Buddha, which was handed down from my ancestors (*opens up the bag fold by fold*). My compound has come several times to convince me to hand it over, but I was reluctant to give it up. Now you take it and hand it over as the contribution of Compound No. 7.

AUNTIE LIU: Grandma Teng, you are truly on our side. But how many ounces of copper can a small bronze Buddha have?

GRANDMA TENG: I know that melon seeds can't fill you, but this is what I have to give.

[*From* Xu Six's *house, sounds of* Spring Happiness *scolding and slapping can be heard again:* "I'm not your mother if I can't manage you!" *The Xu Family door flies open with a loud* "thud." *Little Ni'er rushes out like a mad child. Grandma Teng hurriedly hides the small bronze Buddha in her blouse.*]

LITTLE NI'ER: Auntie Liu! Auntie Liu! My mother forced me to kneel on the washboard again. Please, please adopt me ... (*with a sound of "putong," she kneels down in front of* Auntie Liu, *embraces her legs tightly, and cries loudly*). Mom!

[Spring Happiness *catches up to* Little Ni'er, *and* Xu Six *follows her.*]

XU SIX (*blocks the way of* Spring Happiness): Haven't you done enough?! Haven't you done enough?!

SPRING HAPPINESS: Come back inside!

LITTLE NI'ER: No, I won't go back!

SPRING HAPPINESS: I am your mother! You must listen to me!

LITTLE NI'ER: You're not my mother! My mother was beaten to death by the KMT long ago.

AUNTIE LIU: Little Ni'er, stand up. When the boil is mature, you pop it. You've heard the child call me mother. You've abused this child long enough.

SPRING HAPPINESS: I don't want this child anymore. If you can't rely on your eyeballs, how can you rely on your eye socket?[46] I can't give birth because of her. I would have long since had my own child if I didn't have her!

GRANDMA TENG: Fengzhen, we adopt this child. (*To* Spring Happiness) If you dare beat Little Ni'er again, we'll have you up for justice.

SPRING HAPPINESS: We didn't raise this child on air alone. Give us two thousand pounds of coal and three bags of flour ...

GRANDMA TENG: Nothing else? Have it! Have it all!

XU SIX (*so anxious that he slaps his thighs*): We can't do this! We can't do this!

SPRING HAPPINESS (*can't take her words back, so she tries to find another way*): You can take away this child. But the Liu Family must move out of this compound. I can't stand to let my child call someone else mother!

[*Suddenly the compound quiets down.*]

LITTLE NI'ER: Auntie Liu! Mom! Agree to it! Agree to it! Let's move out of the compound!

LIU JIAXIANG (*walks toward* Spring Happiness): Auntie Xu,[47] let's be good neighbors. You and I can talk it over. How about you move out? Anyway, your house is going to be torn down as we look for cannons . . .

[*The call of the junk buyer floats in and breaks the deadlock.* Little Ring, *wearing a filthy jacket, carrying two baskets on his shoulder pole, appears in front of the street gate. With half of a cigarette on his ear and a small coinlike drum in his hand,* Little Ring *beats the drum while entering the courtyard.*]

SHOPKEEPER SHI: Oh. Is that you, Little Ring?

LITTLE RING (*with a thin voice*): Uncle . . .

LIU JIAXIANG: It's you? Is that really you! Are you out after serving your sentence?

LITTLE RING (*unhappy*): Oh, let unopened pots alone.

SHOPKEEPER SHI: You are . . . are you beating a drum now?

LITTLE RING (*puts down his load and squats*): What else can I do? The fallen phoenix is not as good as a live chicken. Say what you may. I, Little Ring, would have no difficulty managing the Ministry of Finance. But now I am a table rag that wipes up the dirt. . . . Right after I was released, I used to carry a blue cloth bag under my arms and beat a soft drum. I had at least two pretty good trades each month (*seems to bestir himself when he talks about his good times*). By chance I got some priceless scrolls of Tang and Song paintings and an ancient ink stone made in Qing Dynasty. I tricked the bumpkins. Told them they were worthless. I bought them cheap but sold them for a lot more. In one trade I got a stock of cash. Hey! The good times are gone. Everybody now is making steel. . . . How is everyone in the old neighborhood? (*Raises his head*). Hey, don't gather round me like you're watching a monkey show.

SPRING HAPPINESS (*pushes the crowd aside and calls gently*): Little Ring!

LITTLE RING: Spring . . . Six, Auntie Six! (*frightened, stands up*).

SPRING HAPPINESS: What have you come for?

LITTLE RING: To make a Great Leap Forward, I was assigned to collect scrap copper and iron in Small Well Lane, twice a week . . .

SPRING HAPPINESS: You come here. Come here! I have some scrap iron here . . .

LITTLE RING: Where? (*confused and walks over*).

SPRING HAPPINESS (*suddenly raises her hand and slaps* Little Ring *soundly*): You, you bastard! If it wasn't for you, I wouldn't have suffered all these years!

LITTLE RING (*wipes his face*): What on earth is this all about (*wipes his mouth*). My mouth is bleeding. . . . You hit me so hard . . .

SPRING HAPPINESS: Xu Six, give them the child! Let's move out of here! Move out! (*covers her face with two hands, cries, and runs into the house*).

XU SIX (*yelling*): Little Ni'er's mother, we shouldn't move out. . . . The neighbors here are good . . . (*follows* Spring Happiness *into the house*).

LITTLE RING: What have I done? Who knows which cloud has rain in it?

[Third Son Water *enters with blue over-sleeves on his arms and a white apron on his waist, holding a cloth shoe in his right hand. He hasn't been seen for nine years, during which time he has become a peddler of Small Well Lane Store.*]

THIRD SON WATER (*blocks* Little Ring's *way*): Hold on a moment! (*Cries toward the outside*) He is here! Wu Qi, come in! Come here! Don't be scared of him!

[Wu Qi, *grasping a black apron in his left hand and an I-shaped iron anvil (used to repair shoes) in his right hand, enters.*]

WU QI: I am not afraid of him. I've brought my iron anvil with me.

THIRD SON WATER (*stops in front of* Little Ring *and holds the shoe high*): Little Ring! Can you find anyone as evil as yourself? You picked up this completely worn-out shoe somewhere. . . . Wu Qi, what did he tell you?

WU QI: He said to me: "Brother Wu, repair the front and heel of this shoe, and have it soled and heeled. You just make it as sturdy as possible." Since then it has been more than two months, he still hasn't come to take it. . . . If you asked me to repair a pair of shoes, I could have sold them. You left here only one shoe . . .

LITTLE RING: Brother Wu, I was trying to give you an opportunity to improve your skill. At the gathering of heroes, all trades and professions have skillful craftsmen except in the shoe repair business. We have been brothers for years . . . (*tries to escape*).

THIRD SON WATER: Back then, it was you who stirred up trouble and caused Spring Happiness to drink arsenic. Today, I'll teach you a sharp "golden hook" (*sweeps his left leg over* Little Ring). This is called "trip and fall"!

[Little Ring *hurriedly dodges.*]

THIRD SON WATER (*stretches his foot and hooks* Little Ring): This is called "hook."

WU QI: Third Brother, trip him up!

[Third Son Water *deserves to be called "Golden Hook." He easily and quickly trips up* Little Ring, *who falls straight to the ground.*]

THIRD SON WATER: Wu Qi, make him pay! If he pays one penny less, I'll chop him in two. Xu Six, tell Spring Happiness, I have let off her steam for her. But from now on, if she dares to keep treating Little Ni'er badly, I'll take Little Ni'er away from her.

LITTLE RING (*pays*): This was a bad day to go outside.

[Third Son Water, Wu Qi, *and* Little Ring *exit.*]

[Grandma Teng *and* Auntie Liu *lead* Little Ni'er *into the Liu Family's house.*]

AUNTIE SHI (*with envy*): Eh! Fate! "The home without a wutong tree / cannot attract a phoenix."[48]

[Little Mrs., *carrying a blanket, leads* Little Liben, *who wears an old army uniform, into the courtyard.*]

LITTLE MRS.: This is the courtyard.

LITTLE LIBEN (*puts down the string bag and takes a look around*): You explained and explained, I still have no idea where. This is our old shop owner's house. (*The Shi couple hear his words and turn around.*) Uncle Shi!

SHOPKEEPER SHI: Who? Oh! It is Little Liben!

AUNTIE SHI: Hey! After all this time, it is Little Liben. (*Yells*) Auntie Liu, Little Liben is back!

SHOPKEEPER SHI (*looks* Little Liben *up and down*): Good! Good! Little Liben, a high-minded person. Elder niece, your Little Liben is no ordinary man. (*To* Little Liben) You're great! As soon as the Eighth Route Army entered the city, you immediately took out a notebook, which recorded clearly the amounts in each grain store throughout old Beiping. I figured you were a member of the underground Party. You were an apprentice in my shop for two years, but no one knew your real background. Your self-control is really something . . .

LITTLE LIBEN: I wasn't a member of the underground Party but a member of a peripheral organization. I'm still Little Liben, even though I'm a member of the Communist Party now. Is this Er Niu? You're so tall now . . .

ER NIU: Do you know whether Elder Brother "Scarred Squint" has returned, too?

LITTLE LIBEN: Er Niu . . . Elder Brother "Scarred Squint," he, he has long since died . . .

PEOPLE: Ah?

LITTLE LIBEN (*sees the tears in* Er Niu's *eyes, deeply grieved; takes out a small cloth bag from his jacket*): When we first arrived in North Korea, we often talked about our old neighbors in Small Well Lane. Elder Brother "Scarred Squint" used to say: "I don't have a mother and father. But I have a little sister, who is called Er Niu. . . . I still owe Er Niu a lantern. After we defeat the American army and return to Small Well Lane, I'll bring this little lantern to Er Niu." (*He opens up the cloth bag and takes out a small lantern. The lantern is ingeniously constructed and shines with silver light.*) Elder Brother "Scarred Squint" used the wreckage of an American plane to make this lantern for you . . .

[Er Niu *starts to cry.*]

LITTLE LIBEN: He also said that Er Niu likes to play "triangle."⁴⁹ You see, these are all the cigarette wrappers he found for you, Korean wrappers, American wrappers . . . *(turns them over and over in his hands as if fondling a family heirloom).* Keep them, Er Niu, remember Elder Brother "Scarred Squint" . . .

[Er Niu *takes the cigarette wrappers and the lantern with her two hands and treasures them.*]

SHOPKEEPER SHI: Don't be too aggrieved. Little Liben, come inside and take a break . . .

LITTLE LIBEN: No, not now. I need to report to the Housing Office first.

[Little Liben *walks out the street gate. Little Mrs. goes into the house. The others all return to their own homes. Qishi'er, Ma Deqing's adopted son, carrying a cattail bag, enters the courtyard. He wears a military uniform, but there are no red badges on his collar and no red star insignia on his cap.*]

QISHI'ER (*stands in front of the gate*): Does Ma Deqing live here?

[Auntie Jiu *and* Liu Jiaxiang *come out at the same time.*]

LIU JIAXIANG: You are?

QISHI'ER: I am Qishi'er, son of Ma Deqing.

LIU JIAXIANG: Ah. I know you. Please sit down. Auntie Jiu, you go tell Ma Deqing.

[Auntie Jiu *rushes out the gate.*]

QISHI'ER: Uncle, may I ask . . . are you Mr. . . . ?

LIU JIAXIANG: Forget the Mr.! Call me Liu Jiaxiang.

QISHI'ER (*very warm toward* Liu): You are Uncle Liu! I have long known you from my father's letters. Thank you for taking care of my father all these years.

LIU JIAXIANG: Hey. Don't mention it. We are old neighbors. You won't have to leave again?

QISHI'ER (*hangs his head in shame*): I still have to leave. Uncle Liu, you are our friend. I'll tell you the truth. I made a mistake in the Airing of Views . . .⁵⁰

LIU JIAXIANG (*stands up involuntarily and blurts out*): A rightist?

QISHI'ER (*feels peculiarly relaxed after it's put so bluntly*): In fact, I just wanted to give a well-intentioned suggestion. (*Hears footsteps coming hurriedly from outside*) But please don't tell my father, not a word.

[Ma Deqing *and* Auntie Jiu *walk in as if on wings.*]

MA DEQING: Where? Where is my son?

QISHI'ER: Father!

[Little Mrs. *comes out of the inner courtyard.*]

MA DEQING (*face wrinkles in joy*): Qishi'er, come here, come here and meet the neighbors. This is Uncle Liu. (*Proudly*) Take a look, this is my son! A member of the Communist Party and a newspaper reporter. This time, no matter what you say, father and son won't separate again.

QISHI'ER: Father, we still have to separate for a little while . . .

MA DEQING: What's the matter?

QISHI'ER: I was transferred to another post. I am going to the Great Northern Wilderness⁵¹ to help the construction of the border area . . .

MA DEQING: Good! (*doesn't seem to care*). Wherever you go, I'll follow you.

QISHI'ER: No, father, please don't.

MA DEQING: I've got one foot in the grave. If you leave me alone again, I'll just die. Brother Liu, give me the things you kept for me! (*Suddenly realizes that there are many people around them, so he speaks into* Liu Jiaxiang's *ear*) Give me the things you kept for me (*casts a worried look at* Little Mrs.).

LIU JIAXIANG: Brother Ma, you shouldn't leave on the spur of the moment. It will be better to let Qishi'er go there first. After he settles down, then he can come back to take you with him . . .

MA DEQING: That's okay, too (*stroking his son's shoulders and laughing*). I feel proud because of my honorable son. Speaking of his character, he is impeccable. Regarding his political future, he is a member of the Communist Party! Wherever he goes, he will be respected by others. After he gets married, I'll then stay home to play with my grandson. Brother Liu, let's settle this now: No matter where we are, I will invite you to attend my son's wedding. You must come!

LIU JIAXIANG: You bet. I'll be sure to come.

[Qishi'er, *holding* Ma Deqing's *arm, exits.*]

LITTLE MRS. (*suspiciously*): Uncle Liu, isn't it true that Ma Deqing's son is a soldier?

LIU JIAXIANG: Eh. . . . Today I am just wracked with aches and pains . . . (*enters his house*).

[Little Cao *enters the courtyard.*]

LITTLE MRS.: Little Cao, I have just listened to the opinions of the masses about you. But please don't take it to heart . . .

LITTLE CAO: Certainly, "even the blameless can take criticism as another form of encouragement!"[52]

LITTLE MRS.: Someone said that Little Cao has a relative who is a temporary resident and that he was approved for 30 lbs. of rice coupons only because of you . . .

LITTLE CAO: But that is not true. I am wronged!

LITTLE MRS.: I know that. So I corrected them on the spot.

LITTLE CAO: Who? Who really offered this opinion? This isn't because I don't want listen to the views of the masses but because . . .

LITTLE MRS.: Who said that? How can I tell you? (*takes a look at Lius' house*). . . . But remember, I, I don't want to stir up grudges among the old neighbors.

[*Two policemen from the Public Security Office enter the courtyard.*]

POLICEMAN A: Little Cao. Which house?

LITTLE CAO (*points to* Chen Jiuling's *house*): That house.

POLICEMAN B: Chen Jiuling! Chen Jiuling!

[Chen Jiuling, *still sleepy, shuffles out with the backs of his shoes turned in like slippers. Auntie Jiu follows him. The neighbors pour out from their own homes.*]

POLICEMAN A: Are you Chen Jiuling?

CHEN JIULING: Yes, I am. Do you need a hand for the backyard steel furnaces? Let's go to my workplace; my home is too crowded . . .

POLICEMAN B: We are policemen. We are taking you to the Public Security Office to check your background.

CHEN JIULING: Oh. Why me? Why are you taking me? Ask the neighbors, Chen Jiuling does his work. A nail is a nail, and a rivet is a rivet. What I say is what is in my heart . . .

POLICEMAN A: Therefore, we are taking you to confirm your speech at the meeting.

CHEN JIULING: Hey, that speech? I didn't provide that blacklist . . .

AUNTIE JIU (*anxiously*): Comrades, my husband, is a half-wit. He likes talking nonsense.

LITTLE CAO: This is a case involving life and death. You have to tell the truth.

CHEN JIULING (*to* Auntie Jiu): Who is a half-wit? You know nothing. The people's government won't be unjust to a good citizen. I'll go tell them the truth. Let's go.

[Policemen *and* Chen Jiuling *exit;* Auntie Jiu *follows.*]

LITTLE CAO (*to the neighbors in the courtyard*): Don't be confused. The Public Security Office found a person named Chen Jiuling in their files on enemy and collaborationist personnel[53] who was involved in a case of two manslaughters. But there is no such record in our Chen Jiuling's file. The Public Security office thought that perhaps they just have the same name. So they didn't take Chen Jiuling in. But everyone here heard what Chen Jiuling confessed in that meeting. I don't know what will come of all this. Anyway, we shouldn't let Chen Jiuling's case stall our Small Well Lane's Great Leap Forward. The leaders have already decided, in order to double steel production, down comes that house! Up comes the cannon! Tear it down! The district leaders promise to solve the housing problem of the resident whose house is torn down.

SHOPKEEPER SHI: Come on. Move the things out (*goes into* Elder Brother "Scarred Squint"'*s room and takes out his iron ladle*). This is Elder Brother "Scarred Squint"'s ladle to make candy figures. He, died . . . (*doesn't know what to do*).

LITTLE MRS. (*takes the ladle*): If Elder Brother "Scarred Squint" were alive, he would donate it! No matter how valuable the thing is, we shouldn't be reluctant to give it up for the Great Leap Forward.

[*At this moment a " thump" explodes, the house next door has fallen down. Someone is yelling: "Cannon! Cannon! Here it comes!"*]

LITTLE CAO: Compound No. 5 is ahead now! We must get rid of this white flag in our compound.

GRANDMA TENG: Little Cao is right! If we want to make a Great Leap Forward, we must make sacrifices! (*takes out the small bronze Buddha, rubs it with a handkerchief for a last time, and then puts it into the ladle*).

ER NIU (*carrying the little lantern made by* Elder Brother "Scarred Squint," *stops in front of the ladle and says sincerely*): Elder Brother "Scarred Squint," I know you won't blame me. You have sacrificed your life for our country. This is for our country, too. I contribute this lantern (*carefully puts the lantern in the ladle*).

[*The compound suddenly becomes quiet, save for the sound of one piece of metal touching another.* Little Liben *rushes in with a map roll in his hand.*]

LITTLE LIBEN: Comrade Cao! See this map. A sewer pip has been installed under the south house. If there are cannons, they must be buried under the north house . . .

SHOPKEEPER SHI: What? Under the north . . . north house . . .

[*A deafening sound of gongs, drums, and firecrackers pours into the lane again. Someone is yelling, "Small Well Lane succeeded in making steel!"*]

SHOPKEEPER SHI (*gritting his teeth*): Tear it down! Tear down the house! The government will build us a new high-rise after we dig out cannons. My old neighbors, come on!

LITTLE CAO: Right! Eat at the dining hall and live in the high-rises.[54] Communism stands before us!

[*The loudspeaker at the backyard steel furnace site blares "Each Year What Do We Sing?": "The whole country competes to advance. / Everywhere flowers are blooming. / In fifteen years we will surpass old England. / Hey! Together we sing victory! / Everyone is awash in the longing for Communism."*]

[*Sounds of cheering . . .*]

(CURTAIN)

ACT THREE

TIME Early September 1966. It is fall, but the whole of Beijing is still awash in a powerful heat wave. A hard hot wind blows in from who knows where. No one can withstand this hot wind. Nobody actually wants to. Everybody bends with the wind.[55]

PLACE Compound No. 7, Small Well Lane.

SCENE There is no great change in the compound. It is five o'clock in the morning. The streetlights are on. Curtains still cover each window. The whole compound seems not yet awakened from its deep sleep. . . . The street gate is left unlocked. It seems someone got up early and went out already.

   The middle school across the lane is now a temporary guesthouse for Red Guards who have come to Beijing to support the Cultural Revolution.[56] Several windows are broken, and a recently installed loudspeaker stands on the top of the building. Two slogans are written in a slipshod hand on the wall. One is: "Only Permit Leftists to Rebel, Do Not Allow Rightists to Overthrow Heaven!" Another goes: "It's Easy to Move a Mountain, but It's Hard to Shift the Red Guards!"

> [CURTAIN RISES. *In this quiet scene only the distant chiming of the bells at the Beijing Railroad Station float through Small Well Lane. The streetlights flash off. Suddenly the speaker on the school building blares: "The Mao Zedong Thought Propaganda Studio of the Capital Red Guard Military School now commences today's struggle." A musical version of quotations from Chairman Mao*

follows: [57] *"We Communist Party members are like seeds, and the people are like soil . . . " A girl's voice interrupts the broadcasting: "Hey! Hey! No! No! You're playing the wrong side. The other side, the other side. . . . " The music stops. A moment later the speaker delivers strains of "The East Is Red." But, before the singing starts, the music stops again. A male student's voice: "Why? Why did the music stop again . . . ?" A female student's anxious voice: "Turn it off! Turn off the broadcast switch first!" With a "pop" the speaker is turned off. The compound again quiets down. After a while the street gate is pushed open with a slight sound. Auntie Jiu, with an empty string bag in her hand, enters the courtyard in a flurry and rushes directly to the window of the Lius' house.*]

AUNTIE JIU (*lowering her voice*): Auntie Liu. Auntie Liu. Aren't you up? Get up quickly! (*her voice is shaking*).

[*The Lius' curtain is drawn back.* Auntie Liu *walks out while buttoning her blouse.*]

AUNTIE LIU: What's wrong with you? Even your voice is strange.

AUNTIE JIU: My god, they are beating people at the entrance of the lane! A bunch of people are kneeling down there with yin/yang heads.[58] Their heads are split open like melons. . . . I couldn't watch anymore . . .

AUNTIE LIU: Whose family?

AUNTIE JIU: The family in that elegant house. It's said they are landlords and capitalists (*thinking for a while*). I think Wu Qi is kneeling there, too. . . . I'm scared to death. So I didn't even go buy food (*wiping beads of sweat rolling down her forehead*). Auntie Liu, you tell me, what can I do?

AUNTIE LIU: . . . What can you do? You are such a child, you wouldn't listen to my advice. Little Jiu is in prison now, but he is he, you are you. This is clearly written in the "Sixteen Articles":[59] you're not judged only by your family background. You don't have to be so worried.

AUNTIE JIU: These days, my eyelids can't stop jumping.[60] Auntie Liu, our Little Jiu grew up under your nose. He really didn't give the blacklist . . .

Little Mrs. confiscates a suspicious bolt of cloth during the Cultural Revolution (from the stage production).

AUNTIE LIU: The neighbors all know that. Lots of people have the same names in the world. But these days it seems you just can't explain it. Anyway, you could never find another half-wit like him . . .

[*Two Red Guards appear in front of the street gate. They wear old washed-out military uniforms, with red armbands on their arms.*]

RED GUARD A (*yelling loudly when he enters the courtyard*): Who put this couplet[61] on the compound door?

RED GUARD B: Eh? Who did it?

[*Almost every family lifts their curtain corners and peeks out, but nobody dares come outside.*]

RED GUARD A: Why don't I hear anyone speaking?

[*After quite a while, the door of the Shi Family squeaks open, and* Shopkeeper Shi *walks out with fear and trepidation. He's holding a fresh Big Character poster[62] and two copies of his housing certificate.*]

75

SHOPKEEPER SHI (*with trembling lips*): I . . . I . . . I wrote this, you gentlemen . . .

RED GUARD A: The title line you wrote, "Raise Up the Proletariat, Knock Down the Bourgeoisie," is wrong! How can you create without destroying? Change it! "Knock Down the Bourgeoisie, Raise Up the Proletariat." First destroy, then construct!

SHOPKEEPER SHI (*his heart settles back down from his throat*): Right, you said it right. Too right. If you don't destroy, how can you construct? I was blind. I must change it right away . . .

[Red Guards A *and* B *turn and walk out. All the residents of the courtyard heave a sigh of relief.*]

AUNTIE LIU: You are just frightened; your mouth is still trembling . . . (*pointing to the things in* Shopkeeper Shi's *hand*). You . . .

SHOPKEEPER SHI: It's a Big Character poster I wrote. I'm turning the house over to the government. I am sending the title to the Housing Bureau. . . . I've drawn a line[63] (*not knowing how to say it*). "Break with the Ideology of Private Property!" First I'll change the couplets . . . (*returns to his house*).

AUNTIE JIU: Auntie Liu, I have always had another worry. Over the past ten years I have saved extra yarn when I knit woolen clothes for the street knitwear factory. I have knitted all the yarn I have saved into Big Ox's long underwear (*points to the narrow lane with her chin*). You know grand-aunt[64]—she's in charge of that factory. If she searches our house and finds it, won't we be doubly guilty?

AUNTIE LIU (*suddenly remembers*): Hey! I have some extra yarn I saved, too (*sweat rolls down her forehead*). This is not our fault! I tried to return the extra yarn to them, but they didn't want it.

AUNTIE JIU: They won't let you explain that when they come to your house . . .

AUNTIE LIU: Throw them away! Throw them away, that's it. Don't be like a rabbit who is always scared of being shot. Damn it, my heart is pounding, too . . . (*tries to find a way while muttering*). Little Ni'er went to destroy the "four olds,"[65] and "Missy Liu"[66] hasn't come home for a long time. (*Lowering her voice*) Is Big Ox at home?

AUNTIE JIU: Yes, he's home. He isn't qualified to join the Red Guards.

AUNTIE LIU: Ask him to put the yarn you saved into his shoulder bag and go to the suburbs, as far as possible, and throw it away.... By the way, he can take mine with him, too.

[*Auntie Jiu hurries home. A few people are jabbering in Sichuan dialect outside the compound. It's* Little Cao, *who is hosting several Red Guards who have come to Beijing to support the Cultural Revolution. The Red Guards are two males and one female, with their bags on their shoulders and rolled-up banners in their hands. They appear to be fresh off the train.*]

MALE RED GUARD (*speaking in a Sichuan dialect*): Where is the guesthouse for Red Guards?

LITTLE CAO: The building ahead is the guesthouse, the Red Guard Military School. The lodgings there are modest, but you can make do . . .

FEMALE RED GUARD: We don't care whether the lodging is good or bad. We came for revolution. When will Chairman Mao receive us?

LITTLE CAO: In a few days. I'll let you know when I get the notice.

[*The Red Guards leave, but the Sichuan dialect can still be heard from somewhere.*]

AUNTIE LIU: Captain Cao. Captain Cao (*steps forward to greet him*).

LITTLE CAO (*walks into the courtyard. His hands wave like a drum-shaped rattle*): No, no, no. Auntie Liu, don't. Don't call me Captain Cao anymore. I've had to stand down. Now I am only in charge of finding lodgings for Red Guards.

AUNTIE LIU (*whispering*): Are they beating Wu Qi?

LITTLE CAO: Yes. His home was searched, too. He was a puppet policeman. (*Lowering his voice*) His whole family was weeping. They've been exiled to their hometown—Qinglong county in Hebei province, a very poor place.

AUNTIE LIU: Who took the Red Guards there?

LITTLE CAO: Who? Who else? (*holding out his little finger while twitching his mouth to point down the narrow lane*). Auntie Liu, you can know a person's face but not her heart. When she first came to Small Well Lane, she was such a lovely Little Mrs. She always smiled before opening her mouth and had honey on her lips. After I was promoted to captain, she used to lick my boots. But these days she's crazy. She led people to attack Wu Qi . . .

[Shopkeeper Shi, *with ink box and brush pen in his hands, comes out.*]

LITTLE CAO (*immediately raising his voice*): Uncle Shi, have you vacated your house? More and more Red Guards are coming. Schools, hotels, and even bathhouses are full. Some of them now are staying in Zhongnanhai.[67] The leading comrades at the Center tuck their blankets in at night. The newspapers say that they are Chairman Mao's guests and will be billeted in residents' houses if need be.

SHOPKEEPER SHI: Comrade Cao, don't worry. The government wants to use our house; that means the government trusts us. Last night we worked the whole night to vacate the house. It's ready for them to move in!

LITTLE CAO: Good! Uncle Shi, you're great . . .

[Little Cao *exits.* Shopkeeper Shi *goes to change the couplets on the street gate.* Auntie Liu *returns to her home.* Big Ox, *carrying a bulky shoulder bag, comes out of the house with* Auntie Jiu.]

AUNTIE LIU (*opens her door and stretches her head*): Big Ox, Big Ox, come here.

[Big Ox *enters the Lius' house.* Liu Jiaxiang *shuffles out with the backs of his shoes tucked in and a washbasin in his hands. He stops in front of the water tap.*]

LIU JIAXIANG (*finds two bolts of black cloth next to the sink*): Eh? Whose bolts of cloth?

[Auntie Jiu *and* Auntie Liu *walk out when they hear the news. They stare blankly at the cloth.* Shopkeeper Shi *also hurries over. The ink box in his hands is shaking.*]

LIU JIAXIANG (*puts down the washbasin and takes the cloth in his arms*): "Golden Deer" brand? Wow, these bolts must be old! Brother

Shi, last night you vacated your house. Did you forget these two bolts of cloth?

SHOPKEEPER SHI (*his fears coming true*): No! Brother Liu, how can they be ours! You should know that our family property doesn't amount to such substantial resources. We have long since spent all of it . . .

[Auntie Shi *bursts open the door and walks out.*]

AUNTIE SHI: Brother Liu, at this critical moment your words must be: "a nail is a nail, and a rivet is a rivet." This is a case of life and death. The old neighbors know us as clear as a mirror. We are not people who take advantage of others' misfortunes.

[Little Mrs. *enters the courtyard with a serene look.*]

LIU JIAXIANG: If nobody wants them, I'll take them home.

LITTLE MRS. (*sneering*): Our compound, to tell an unpleasant truth, is a small temple hiding a big god (*stares at the cloth*). Did it fly in from other compounds? What kind of background does this person have, if he has saved so much cloth in his house? He must have been an exploiter back then, isn't it crystal clear? When our Little Liben was an apprentice in his shop, he once broke a bowl and was forced to use a bamboo strainer to eat all his meals!

SHOPKEEPER SHI: Big Sister (*flattering the younger woman*). I did hire one or two shop assistants. But these bolts of cloth are truly not mine. I was a small shopkeeper; that is a class that allies with the Five Red Classes . . .[68]

LITTLE MRS. (*carries the cloth under her arm*): We must find out whose bolts these are (*enters the inner courtyard*).

LIU JIAXIANG: Great, more trouble . . .

AUNTIE SHI (*to* Shopkeeper Shi): Why don't you go call Zengfu immediately . . . (*faces* Auntie Liu *but actually throwing words toward the inner courtyard*). I am almost fifty years old and can't get pregnant. Therefore, we adopted a son of Reifeng's old brother. When you see our adopted son, then you will know what kind of background we have.

[Shopkeeper Shi *exits.*]

AUNTIE LIU (*open her house's door*): Big Ox! Be a good boy. Sorry to have given you so much trouble (*tries to think of a tale to spin to Auntie Shi*). Our Er Niu has just given birth! Today she is discharged from the hospital. I made a cape for my "tiny tot." (*Enjoins* Big Ox) Come home as soon as possible.

[Big Ox, *carrying the bulky shoulder bag, runs out of the street gate. Two Red Guards,* Big Horse, *and* Little Song, *from the street knitwear factory, escort* Wu Qi *into the courtyard.*]

WU QI (*crying*): Old neighbors! Please be fair!

[*All the people living in the compound come out.*]

WU QI: It's true, I worked as a KMT policeman before liberation. But I was only a sergeant! In addition, I saved the life of a child whose parents were in the Eighth Route Army . . .

LITTLE MRS.: A mere verbal statement is no guarantee. Where is that child?

WU QI: I put him in front of Auntie Liu's door. I know Auntie Liu is a kind person and would adopt him. I was a son of a bitch! If I had known what would happen today, I would have done anything—pawn my pants and sell my shirt—to bring him up . . .

LITTLE MRS.: Don't waste your breath! Where is the child?

WU QI: He was kidnapped . . .

BIG HORSE: Perhaps he was murdered by you. You are doubly bad. Go!

AUNTIE LIU: Wait a minute! (*blocking their way*). Little Sturdy was taken by kidnappers. Third Son Water was an eyewitness. Grandma Teng also knows this affair.

[Er Niu, *cradling her newborn baby—"little tot"—leads* Grandma Teng *by the arm into the courtyard.*]

GRANDMA TENG: What cause do you have to struggle Wu Qi? Little Sturdy really was brought home by Wu Qi. It was a time of chaos; the kidnapping was unavoidable. When Bi Wu was executed, he must have made a confession. The government should have a record of this. If you send Wu Qi away, what will become of his children and wife?

LITTLE MRS.: Grandma Teng, don't talk like that. Could an old society cop really save the life of a good child? Is it possible? Little Sturdy is the descendant of a revolutionary martyr. Lost? Lost where? (*glances at* Auntie Liu). How was it your biological children weren't lost? . . . Wu Qi not only has historical problems; he is also an active counterrevolutionary. Little Song, take him away.

[*The charge "active counterrevolutionary" shuts everyone up completely.*]

WU QI: My old neighbors, since you have said these fair-minded words, Wu Qi is not condemned to an empty life. Wu Qi bows to you . . .

LITTLE MRS.: Big Horse, come over to my house.

[Little Song *drags* Wu Qi *away.* Little Liben, *who had been watching these events through a wrinkled brow, follows after* Little Mrs. *to his house.*]

ER NIU: Mother, we can't call the kid "Little Tot" forever. He needs a proper name.

LIU JIAXIANG: He wasn't born at the right time. He just came to add more chaos, really. I reckon, "Adding Chaos" fits . . .

GRANDMA TENG: You're kidding! I can't take anymore aggravation. I'm sixty-nine years old this year. Call him "Little Six Nine."

[*People all return to their homes. A flatbed three-wheeled bicycle stops at the courtyard gate.* Third Son Water *comes in carrying a basket of eggs.*]

THIRD SON WATER (*wiping sweat*): Er Niu's mother, here are some eggs. Tell Er Niu these are summer eggs. You have to use them now. . . . If you need me, just let me know. I must get back to my cart (*turns to leave*).

[Shopkeeper Shi *enters the courtyard.*]

SHOPKEEPER SHI (*putting on a happy and relaxed face*): Auntie Liu, Third Brother, I have turned in the house deed. After you become proletarian your heart feels just light and bright. . . . (*Suddenly finding no one around, walks over and begs in a low voice*) Auntie, please accept those two bolts of cloth as your own. They are mine, but you have a good class background and have no historical problems.[69] I've hired labor, eaten the food of the exploiter …

AUNTIE LIU: Actually I am also like a clay idol fording a river[70] … (*strengthening herself*). Okay, I'll take these two bolts for you …

SHOPKEEPER SHI: If you help me this time, I will never forget what you have done for me …

THIRD SON WATER: Where is the cloth? I'll take it. Just after liberation, money lost its value; everybody collected goods instead of money then (*continues to talk while leaving*). It's nothing (*exits*).

[Ma Deqing, *who works at the local telephone station,*[71] *comes in.*]

MA DEQING (*intentionally raising his voice*): Brother Shi! Brother Shi! Your phone call (*sees* Shopkeeper Shi *twitching his mouth to point down the narrow lane; understands tacitly. He shuffles toward the inner courtyard, shouting loudly*). Brother Shi! Your phone call! It's your nephew's call from the AIR FORCE. He said he's coming to see you! That's all he said. Oh, so you have a nephew who's in the LIBERATION ARMY!

SHOPKEEPER SHI: Yes, yes. Thank you very much.

[*As* Ma Deqing *is about to leave,* Big Horse, *with two blots of black cloth on his shoulder, follows* Little Mrs. *out of the inner courtyard.*]

LITTLE MRS.: Ma Deqing, wait a moment!

MA DEQING: Are you talking to me?

LITTLE MRS.: Yes, you. (*With a mild tone*) You are educated and must know the leaders' policies.

MA DEQING: I know …

LITTLE MRS.: Newspapers have explained it all very well: the Cultural Revolution is like a fight between opposing armies. If I can't beat you, then you will beat me. There is no question of compromise …

MA DEQING: You're right. Leftists, rightists …

LITTLE MRS.: Your problems, we know all about them. Come, make a confession.

MA DEQING: I confess, I confess it all.... (*Looks at* Shopkeeper Shi) Older Brother, I am really sorry. (*Turns to* Little Mrs.) The phone call I just mentioned was totally made-up.... It's Brother Shi who asked me to say that ...

AUNTIE SHI (*suddenly gives* Shopkeeper Shi *a powerful punch and scolds him*): This is all your fault! You always mess things up! (*rushes into their house, crying*).

LITTLE MRS. (*stares blankly for a little while, not knowing what* Ma Deqing *was talking about but immediately calms down*): Slowly. Confess it clearly.

MA DEQING: Last night Brother Shi told me that during these days, if you could have a relative who was a soldier pay a visit to your house, you would certainly look good, so that you won't have to worry about the neighbors' suspicions about your family background ...

SHOPKEEPER SHI (*takes over and carries forward*): Brother Ma. Let me finish the confession. Confessing myself may mitigate my sins.... I have a nephew who sells fish in a food market. I asked him to wear a borrowed army uniform and come to have lunch with us today ...

BIG HORSE (*can't hold back his laughing to* Ma Deqing): Blockhead, we were not asking you about that.

MA DEQING and SHOPKEEPER SHI (*at the same time*): What?

LITTLE MRS.: Big Horse, keep your moth shut! Ma Deqing, you still have one more thing you haven't confessed.

MA DEQING: Thing, one more thing? What is that ...

LITTLE MRS.: I'll give you one more hint. In 1958, before your son, a rightist, left, you tried to follow him and asked Liu Jiaxiang to.... Do you want me to continue?

LIU JIAXIANG (*has been watching the fun with his hands clasped behind his back, suddenly understands*): Hey! Older niece, you really have a good memory. (*Sarcastically*) Brother Ma, you do have one more thing. Do you still want to get by under false pretenses? (*holding up his thumb aimed at* Little Mrs.). Older niece, this time you really caught a big one (*returns home*).

MA DEQING (*mistakes* Liu Jiaxiang's *mischief and bursts out*): Damn it, nobody can be fucking trusted these days! (*squats down with rage*).

LIU JIAXIANG (*carefully carries out a small wooden box wrapped in apricot yellow satin*): Take a look, Brother Ma, this is the treasure they want from you . . .

LITTLE MRS.: Big Horse, take it.

MA DEQING (*suddenly stands up*): Father of Er Niu, we have a long-standing friendship over many years. I can't believe that you, too, have no backbone. If you have no benevolence [ren], then I have no righteousness [yi].[72] What about that time you said that the Cultural Revolution is like a household that can't keep together. The eldest son steals a carving knife from the old man, the younger son a rolling pin. The two brothers battle to death! Only the timid fool . . . (*trembling with rage*).

LIU JIAXIANG (*finds what was make-believe has become reality, also becomes anxious*): Brother Ma, Brother Ma. What's wrong with you? I am making fun of them. Why did you hit me?

MA DEQING: You're making fun of them? (*snatches the packet and opens the cloth wrapper with trembling hands*). My old neighbors, you all knew that my uncle was a eunuch. What could he live off after he left the palace? He stole the box of secret prescriptions from the Court Medicine Department. Down to my generation I, too, have no family and children. I adopted a son, but he was labeled a Rightist. (*Points to the box*) I rely on these for the rest of my life. (*Takes out the prescriptions and shakes them*) These are money. These are the money to pay for my coffin!

LIU JIAXIANG: What on earth is this all about? (*To* Little Mrs.) Just tell me what case can you frame against Ma Deqing with these few secret prescriptions? I hid them. I'll take responsibility for it.

LITTLE MRS.: Are you taking responsibility for it? Based on what Ma Deqing has just confessed, what charge do you deserve?

BIG HORSE: Opposing the Great Cultural Revolution! Active counterrevolutionary!

MA DEQING (*cools down and starts to regret what he has said*): I am an old man and have a bad memory. I probably misunderstood what Liu Jiaxiang said . . .

LIU JIAXIANG: Brother Ma, no need for regrets. (*Turns toward* Little Mrs. *and continues joking and cursing*) Older Nephew's wife, what you want is to put your Uncle Liu to shame, don't you? How about this, I write my guilt on a piece of paper and put it at the entrance of the lane. What do you say?

LITTLE MRS. (*can't find the words, turns to* Ma Deqing): You go back first.

[Ma Deqing *exits.*]

LIU JIAXIANG: Just say yes or no. Shaking your head means no, and nodding your head means yes. If you say no words, that means you agree with it! Okay, I am going to do it! (*enters his house*).

[*Just then* Shopkeeper Shi's *nephew* Zhengfu, *wearing an army uniform, enters the courtyard.*]

ZHENGFU: Uncle! Are you busy? (*sees* Shopkeeper Shi *saying nothing, continues to play his role*). The army combat readiness is in full swing, and I had a hard time getting this half-day off. The leading cadre asked me if this is your uncle, the old comrade who came to our military unit before. He also said that your uncle is an honest person (*uneasily takes off his service cap*). Where is my Auntie? (*wipes sweat from his forehead*).

BIG HORSE (*walks over*): What military unit do you serve with?

ZHENGFU: Air force . . .

BIG HORSE (*sniffs about*): Why do I smell the scent of salt fish on you? Are you an officer in the navy?

[Auntie Shi *suddenly rushes out of the house.*]

AUNTIE SHI: Zhengfu! Run! They know everything!

LITTLE MRS.: Where can you escape to?

BIG HORSE: Air force? You sell fish at the food market. You always shortchange customers. Now you pretend to be a member of the People's Liberation Army. Where did you steal this uniform? Confess!

ZHENGFU (*blaming* Shopkeeper Shi): This is all your fault! You are full of rotten ideas. Even when telling the truth, I mumble. You insisted on my telling a lie. Those words I practiced again and again last night. These days if I don't get the weight wrong, I give the wrong change . . .

LITTLE MRS.: Big Horse, don't waste time on him. Take him to his work unit.

[Zhengfu, *following* Big Horse, *exits.*]

AUNTIE SHI (*scolds* Shopkeeper Shi): You are so smart! We adopted this son with great difficulty; now you get him into this trouble. How are you going to explain this to your older brother?

LITTLE MRS.: Everybody has seen what happened. How complicated the class struggle is in our compound. Openly, secretly, inside, outside . . . simply another petty "Three Family Village"[73] (*exits the courtyard*).

[Liu Jiaxiang *comes out with a large piece of paper in his hand.*]

LIU JIAXIANG: Brother Shi, listen to what I have written! (*Reads paper*) "Liu Jiaxiang, male, fifty-two-year-old. He likes joking around and almost joined the 'Yi guan dao.'"[74] The following are included in a bracket: "When I heard that a Taoist priest must be a vegetarian, I returned home before I got to the monastery. How can I be a vegetarian?" end of bracket . . .

SHOPKEEPER SHI: Brother Liu, I have already lost my mind from worry, and you are still in the mood to crack jokes . . .

[Chen Jiuling *unexpectedly appears by the front of the street gate. He wears a creased yellowish-brown shirt and pants and green tennis shoes without socks.*]

CHEN JIULING (*with joy and in a loud voice*): Uncle! How are you doing! Auntie!

AUNTIE JIU: You, why did you come back today? God, but don't you know how to choose the time?

AUNTIE LIU: Little Jiu, why did you come back?

SHOPKEEPER SHI: Escaped? Go surrender yourself to the police immediately.

CHEN JIULING: Escaped? What are you talking about. Chen Jiuling is always a great fellow no matter where he is. There is only one year left before I'm released—why should I escape? The Rebel Faction tossed us back home. Even the government now listens to what the Rebel Faction demands. How can I, Chen Jiuling, not listen to them? This is no joke.

[Little Cao *enters the courtyard. People still call him "Captain Cao."*]

CHEN JIULING: Little Cao! What? You're a captain now? You're fantastic. Remember these words in your heart: a person must have a good heart. Others can be unfair to you, but you should never ever be unfair to others.

LITTLE CAO: Little Jiu, how did you come back?

CHEN JIULING: The Rebel Faction tossed us back. I'm not kidding. All inmates were tossed out. They wouldn't let anyone stay.

LITTLE CAO: You may be telling the truth. But how about this—first you follow me to register at the police station here. We'll then contact the Xinjiang Labor Farm to confirm what has happened. Before we receive the answer from your labor farm, you have to stay in the detention house.

CHEN JIULING: That's fine. Chen Jiuling is always a good fellow.

[*As* Chen Jiuling *and* Little Cao *are going to leave,* Little Ring, *looking triumphant, enters while muttering. He wears a dirty gray shirt and a pair of very old military pants and a PLA green cap on his head. His clothes and cap are completely mismatched.*]

LITTLE RING: Oh? Little Jiu.

CHEN JIULING: Little Ring!

LITTLE RING (*looks* Chen Jiuling *up and down*): Wearing khaki shirt and pants? What's going on? Menfolk . . . you have escaped! Haven't you? (*Making fun of* Chen) The proletarian dictatorship spreads a dragnet, so where can you run to?

LIU JIAXIANG (*ironically*): Dragnet? The net size is still too big. If the size was a little bit tighter, you wouldn't have had a chance to live tastefully outside of the dragnet . . .

CHEN JIULING: Little Ring, one should follow the decent path. Otherwise, sooner or later he'll commit a crime . . .

LITTLE CAO: Chen Jiuling, hold your speeches. Let's go.

CHEN JIULING: Let's go (*but must finish his words*). Little Ring, you haven't committed a crime so far, but, if you do, it will certainly be a big one . . . (*following* Little Cao, *exits*).

LITTLE RING (*disdains the thought of* Chen's *words*): This guy, his stomach is full of shit. (*Turns to* Liu Jiaxiang) Brother Liu! And you? You have lived so many years in vain. You have never found the right temple to serve. Who can imagine that Little Ring is still able to have such good luck? If Fortune-teller Yang were still alive, I would go ask him my fortune . . . (*takes out a creased red armband*). Take a look . . .

LIU JIAXIANG: You? Little Ring, someone like you can join the Red Guards?

LITTLE RING (*slips the armband into his pocket*): The Red Guards won't let me in. I have a record following my ass. I joined the "Red Peripheral Organization." (*Glowing with excitement*) Brother Liu, let me tell you: A person living in this world always wants to enjoy comfort, but, if you want to be comfortable, it is then impossible to avoid committing some wrongdoing. This is a truth, isn't it? But remember I have never gone too far. Little Ring's problems are in the category of "contradictions among the people."[75] So, if someone dares to make trouble for me, I won't go along.

SHOPKEEPER SHI: Today, who are you going to go along with . . . ?

LITTLE RING: I came to look for Little Liben. At the beginning of the Cultural Revolution, he was a member of the Work Team in my work unit. Even a person like him picked on me? Is Little Ring a ripe persimmon? Not a fucking chance. At Beijing University, Zhang Chengxian[76] has already been discharged from his post. I'll teach him a lesson. (*Yelling*) Little Liben! (*Suddenly remembers something and asks* Liu Jiaxiang) Is his wife at home?

LIU JIAXIANG: No, she isn't.

LITTLE RING: Not at home? If she isn't at home, I'll wait for a while.

[Little Mrs., *with Big Ox's shoulder bag in her left hand leading* Big Ox *by her right hand, enters the courtyard.*]

LITTLE MRS. (*stops in front of* Auntie Liu *and* Auntie Jiu): Big Ox, you are a good boy. You say it yourself.

BIG OX (*shrinks back*): Say what? What have I said? I didn't say anything . . .

LITTLE MRS.: Be a good boy. What did you just tell me? Isn't it that your mother asked you to throw this yarn away into the city canals? This is nice wool. Why do you want to throw it away? If you want to be a Red Guard, then you must make a clean break with your family . . .

BIG OX: I ran to the Dragon Lake with my shoulder bag. I couldn't stop to wonder if I was being followed. . . . My father was a KMT soldier before liberation; I shouldn't have helped them . . .

LITTLE MRS.: Good. Good boy. Hmm. Someone is already filled with apprehension by the Red Guards' revolutionary actions.

AUNTIE JIU: Me, I'm not trembling with fear. I got a cold yesterday, so I feel cold now . . .

AUNTIE LIU: This yarn was saved over the years as we knit woolen clothes, but they didn't want it. Actually we don't need to hide it . . .

[Little Song, *carrying two bolts of black cloth on his shoulder, along with* Big Horse, *who carries a dozen paper strip seals, enters the courtyard.*]

BIG HORSE (*fierce in appearance*): Shi Ruifeng! Shi Reifeng!

SHOPKEEPER SHI (*his legs begin to shake*): What are you going to do? Search . . . search my house?

BIG HORSE (*to* Little Mrs.): Should we begin to search his house now?

[*Someone lets out the roar of a lion outside:* "Get out of my way!" Third Son Water *separates the people gathered round and strides through the gate.*]

THIRD SON WATER: What are you doing here? Saving two bolts of cloth doesn't make a person a capitalist. Don't you know the law? To tell you the truth, the bolts are mine. Talk to *me* if you have questions.

LITTLE MRS.: Yours?

LITTLE RING (*standing up*): Hey! This must be "Golden Hook"? You're still ready to take up the cudgels for the little guy. You should consult the almanac to see if your timing is right (*moves over to touch the bolts and then brushes the dust off his hands*). Yep, these two bolts are Third Son Water's. Shi Chuanxiang was the local tyrant controlling the shit and piss trade.[77] You were the local tyrant controlling the delivery of water. All these years Third Son Water never bothered to carry the bolts of cloth to the recycle station. All the bolts have been eaten by insects and are Golden Deer brand . . .

PEOPLE: Little Ring! You are talking nonsense!

[Big Horse *and* Little Song *suddenly grab* Third Son Water's *arms.*]

THIRD SON WATER (*shakes his wrists with the roar of a lion*): Let go! (*throws the two away*). Do you truly want to start a fight? You are no match for me even if you have two more accomplices. (*Points to* Little Mrs.) I feel regret for Little Liben. He is such an honest and kind man. How can he take a bitch like you to be his wife?!

LITTLE RING (*after hearing* Little Liben's *name, narrows his eyes to look at* Little Mrs., *and the truth suddenly dawns on him; he turns around and cries out*): Little Liben! Wang Baode! Comrade Wang Baode!

[Little Liben *comes out from the narrow lane.*]

LITTLE LIBEN: Little Ring? (*knits his brow with disgust*).

LITTLE RING: So that's why can't I find you at the work unit. You've hidden yourself at home.

LITTLE LIBEN: Every day you go to the work unit to cause trouble, so nobody can work there anymore. Yes, the Work Team[78] stood on the wrong side and led the campaign in the wrong direction, but we didn't treat you badly!

LITTLE RING: Let's not talk about that now. (*Speaks with tone of a judge*) Today I only ask you one question: Did you come to our recycle station to lead revolution or commit adultery?

LITTLE LIBEN (*anxiously*): What have you spun wild yarns about?

LITTLE RING (*keeps nailing* Little Liben *down*): Don't pretend to be naive! Every night you talked with the girl who works in the dining hall until two or three o'clock. She's a good-looking girl. But you are a cadre and have a wife at home. What can you do now? That girl now feels nauseous whenever she eats food and looks around the world to buy sour cherry . . .[79]

LITTLE LIBEN (*can't clean himself even if he jumps into the Yellow River; puffs and blows with rage*): You, you . . .

LITTLE MRS. (*rushes to* Little Liben *furiously*): Now I know what you are, you . . .

LITTLE LIBEN (*thumps his thigh*): It's not true! It's not true!

[Little Mrs. *runs into the narrow lane with her hands covering her face.*]

LITTLE RING (*pretends to be stupid*): This woman is? Is this woman your wife? (*Seems to feel regret*) Oh dear, if I had known. . . . Hey! I've caused you trouble. . . . I am just so indignant about . . .

LITTLE LIBEN (*points at* Little Ring): All right. Little Ring. I am no match for you! You are great; you are just great (*turns around to chase after* Little Mrs.).

[Big Horse *and* Little Song *also follow him to run into the inner courtyard.*]

SHOPKEEPER SHI (*moves closer*): Little Ring, is this true?

LITTLE RING (*lights his cigarette with a flourish*): No, it's all just a story. Today I've taught him a lesson . . .

LIU JIAXIANG: Little Ring, you devil, you bite whoever you can catch.

AUNTIE SHI: That's just as it should be: Justice!

[Little Cao *rushes in.*]

LITTLE CAO: Third Uncle! Old neighbors! Hurry! Uncle Ma has stopped breathing. Phlegm or something is blocking his throat!

THIRD SON WATER: Hurry up and find a flatbed cycle!

[*Everyone in the compound hurries out of the gate. People are shouting:* "*Hurry! Don't wait!*" *At the same time,* Little Mrs.'s *sad crying pours out from the inner courtyard.*]

[*The speakers on the roof of the school begin to broadcast the lead article from the July 1966* Red Flag.[80] *But because of the hubbub in the courtyard and also the increased noise from the speakers, we can only hear the reading disjointedly:* "*. . . this campaign must . . . deep soul . . . problems . . . overcome the 'four olds' and foster the 'four news' . . .*"[81]]

(CURTAIN)

ACT FOUR

TIME October 8, 1976, late afternoon. The Gang of Four has been arrested.[82] But the news hasn't spread around Beijing and Small Well Lane yet. Even the people who have served as hatchet men for the Gang of Four are still in the dark.

PLACE Compound No. 7, Small Well Lane.

SCENE Fall seems to have come earlier this year. The old *chun* tree in front of the compound has already turned yellow. The leaves are falling and rolling in the wind, with a rustling sound. The bare branches of the tree oppressively blot out the sky above the compound. The sky is overcast. Leaden clouds like huge millstones push down from the high sky upon the residents of Small Well Lane. The terrible Tangshan earthquake two months ago destroyed all of Tangshan and shook Beijing.[83] The arch over the street gate was cracked by the shock of earthquake, and in the middle of the courtyard the wall in front of the narrow lane fell in, leaving a yard wide gap in it now.

One side of the Lius' house has collapsed; several pieces of plastic sheeting and asphalt felts manage to keep out the cold wind and rain. On the courtyard wall, here and there, are strips of paper on which is written, "Man can conquer nature," and some colorful posters explaining earthquakes. Time has passed, and circumstances have changed, and the strips roll up their corners in the wind.

In the distance there is an obscure crack in the wall of the middle school. On top of the old slogan is a new horizontal one: "Following Chairman Mao's teaching, Carry on the Proletarian Revolution!"

[CURTAIN RISES. *Calm in the courtyard. Beneath the hallway an old stainless steel pot cover hung on the wall taps against the pillar making a tinkling sound. From the radio in the Shi family house wafts the sounds of Yang Chunxia's singing from "Cuckoo Mountain."*[84] *The door of the Liu household opens.* Auntie Jiu *comes out carrying a folded set of linens and quilt cover, going to her house.* Auntie Shi, *wearing a black armband (mourning Chairman Mao's death from September 1976), carries a cookie box into the courtyard.*]

AUNTIE SHI (*stepping forward to meet* Auntie Jiu): Auntie Jiu, you are . . . ?

AUNTIE JIU: I am helping Auntie Liu to make a cotton-wadded quilt for the wedding of Missy Liu [Auntie Liu's son] and Little Ni'er.

AUNTIE SHI (*suddenly*): Good god! You've taken off your black armband!

AUNTIE JIU: How can I wear mourning when preparing for a wedding? Furthermore, it's already been a month . . .

AUNTIE SHI: Today is the eighth. It won't be a month until tomorrow. Did you hear that last week a wedding banquet in the flower market was destroyed by the Workers' Militia? They said that it has been less than a month since our great leader passed away, why did you choose this mourning to take a wife in . . .

AUNTIE JIU: Auntie Liu doesn't want to have a wedding banquet! She is actually pretending to be happy . . . (*showing sympathy*). Er Niu has been arrested and divorced. Uncle Liu had his leg squashed in the earthquake and is still in the hospital. You say . . .

AUNTIE SHI: The weasel specializes in biting sick duck. Anyway, if that grand-aunt hadn't played a dirty trick and arranged to dig an air raid shelter under the Lius' house, it wouldn't have collapsed in the earthquake! I am worried that something might happen to Auntie Liu. These days she seems always lost in her own thoughts.

AUNTIE JIU: It is because she misses Six Nine terribly. The court gave Six Nine to his father. This verdict breaks Auntie Liu's heart. Her son-in-law even quit his job in Beijing and moved back to Baotou . . .

[*The pot cover in the corridor continues to make noise. Shi's door opens with a bang.* Shopkeeper Shi, *panting with rage, carrying a small transistor radio, rushes out.*]

A lonely alley.

AUNTIE SHI (*suddenly recalls*): Today when I took the Route No. 5 bus, I saw a child standing in front of the Taoranting Park. He looked so much like Little Six Nine. I asked myself, would it be possible that this child was Little Six Nine?

AUNTIE JIU: Perhaps your eyes tricked you . . .

SHOPKEEPER SHI (*unnamable anger eats him; he tears off the pot cover harshly and hurls it on the coal pile*): Damn! Who got this bastard cover and hung it here to bother people?! (*To Auntie Shi*) Whenever you hear wind, you think it will rain. There are more than one thousand miles from Baotou to Beijing. A ten-year-old child came here by himself? . . . Nonsense!

AUNTIE SHI: I wasn't talking to you. (*Touches the quilt cover in Auntie Jiu's hands*) Cotton fabric? Auntie Liu takes a daughter-in-law; I ought to give a hand. But, I am a childless person and shouldn't touch a dowry. You are a lucky person; you have a son . . .

SHOPKEEPER SHI: Don't talk nonsense here. Little Jiu is still in jail. What luck does Auntie Jiu have? (*doesn't know that* Auntie Liu *has walked out*). Is a wedding always a happy time? Auntie Liu's heart is steeped in her tears. Little Ni'er and Missy Liu are still in the countryside. After they get married, they'll lose the chance to return to Beijing . . . (*suddenly sees* Auntie Liu *and stops talking*).

AUNTIE SHI (*steps forward*): Auntie Liu, great happiness to you . . .

SHOPKEEPER SHI: Auntie Liu, great happiness . . . (*his strained smile is even more ugly than crying*).

AUNTIE LIU (*smiles in sadness*): Happy together, happy together . . .

AUNTIE SHI: Auntie Liu, don't worry too much. Our kids are honest. As soon as Chairman Mao waved his hand, they went to the countryside. One day Chairman Mao will wave his hand again, and our children will return to Beijing . . .

SHOPKEEPER SHI: What can I say to you! (*Enters his house while muttering*) Chairman Mao has passed away for almost a month. . . . With a wave of his hand . . .

[Auntie Jiu *feels low; she carries the quilt back to her home.*]

AUNTIE SHI (*knows that she hasn't cheered* Auntie Liu *up; quickly changes the topic and holds up the cookie box in her hand*): Auntie Liu, I won't be going to the hospital to see Brother Liu. Here I bought some cookies for him . . .

AUNTIE LIU: You have gone to such expense again . . .

AUNTIE SHI: Don't mention it! These are regular folks cookies . . .

AUNTIE LIU: Brother Shi, could you please read this letter? Little Ni'er has gone to the market, and Missy Liu went to change cloth coupons . . .[85]

SHOPKEEPER SHI (*takes over the letter*): From Baotou! Perhaps this letter is from your son-in-law . . .

AUNTIE LIU: He and Er Niu were divorced. He isn't my son-in-law anymore . . .

SHOPKEEPER SHI (*opens the letter*): Auntie Liu, it's from your son-in-law! The letter says that Six Nine has left home since the morning of the second and hasn't returned. He wondered if Six Nine has come here.

AUNTIE LIU: Ah! Six Nine?

AUNTIE SHI: What did I just say! The child I saw in front of the Taoranting Park probably was Six Nine!

SHOPKEEPER SHI (*not willing to listen*): You are talking nonsense again! Auntie Liu, our Six Nine has a sensitive heart. Since Er Niu was arrested; he has been having troubles with his mind. It is impossible for him to come to Beijing by himself. I say, let's first make a long distance phone call to Baotou to ask what has happened . . .

[Auntie Liu *is about to cry. At this moment Liu Guizhi*—Little Ni'er—*enters with an empty string bag in her hand.*]

LITTLE NI'ER: Mom . . .

AUNTIE LIU (*raises her head*): You have returned! Where is the kerosene stove?

LITTLE NI'ER (*replies timidly*): I didn't buy it. . . . Mother, please don't be angry with me. We have been to the countryside for so many years. Each year you sent money to support us. . . . Why not save the money we can save? For generations the village people have never had a kerosene stove. . . . As for me and Missy Liu's wedding, we only want to send a bag of candy to each house of the old neighbors. That's all. No banquet . . .

AUNTIE LIU (*stubbornly*): Be a good child, listen to what Mom says! If I don't prepare your dowry well, I'll feel shamed before your biological parents . . .

[*Along with a squeaky sound of the street gate,* Little Six Nine, *in dirty clothes, enters the courtyard. His pocket is bulging with something inside.*]

AUNTIE SHI (*is the first one to see* Little Six Nine): Six Nine?

AUNTIE LIU (*surprised*): Six Nine!?

LITTLE SIX NINE: Grandma! (*throws himself into* Auntie Liu's *arms, weeping*).

AUNTIE LIU (*her heart is full of grief*): Good boy. Don't cry (*wipes the child's tears*). How did you come here?

LITTLE SIX NINE (*says stubbornly while sobbing*): I didn't cry. I never cry. I took the train. They tossed me out of the train every time they found I didn't have a ticket. But I waited for the next train . . .

(*by accident the things in his pocket fall out. They are a pair of glasses and a key chain. He hurriedly reaches to pick them up*).

AUNTIE LIU (*picks up the glasses*): Glasses?

LITTLE SIX NINE: . . . I brought them for my mom. My mom can't correct students' work without this pair of glasses.

AUNTIE LIU: What is this key chain for?

[Little Six Nine *grasps the keys and holds them in front of his chest.*]

AUNTIE SHI: Six Nine, have you been to Taoranting Park?

LITTLE SIX NINE (*looks flustered*): How do you know that? Grandma Shi, please don't tell anyone. If you tell someone else, I won't be able to save my mom . . .

PEOPLE: Save your mother?

LITTLE SIX NINE (*firmly*): Save my mom! My mom is a good person! I know where the prison is. The prison is on the west side of Taoranting Park, on Zixin Road . . . (*holds up the keys*). Grandma, I collected these keys . . .

AUNTIE SHI: Be a good boy, stop talking nonsense. (*To* Auntie Liu) Look at the beads of sweat on his forehead. He's not well. Ruifeng, hurry and make a bowl of sugar water for Six Nine . . .

SHOPKEEPER SHI (*stops in front of his house*): Six Nine! Come to Grandpa Shi's house! (*To* Auntie Shi) Hey! You bring the child here!

[Auntie Shi, *leading* Little Six Nine, *follows her husband into the house. As* Auntie Liu *and* Little Ni'er *are also walking to the Shis' house,* Xu Six *carries in a medium-sized fruit basket. He has been living away from Small Well Lane for eighteen years. He is now an old man in his sixties.*]

XU SIX (*feels shame and calls with a hesitating voice*): Auntie Liu . . .

AUNTIE LIU: Xu Six? Why did you come? Guizhi, your father is here. Come here. Say hello. Say hello to your father.

XU SIX (*deeply touched*): Little Ni'er, go ahead and scold me—your dad. But don't ignore me . . . your father is a worthless wretch . . .

LITTLE NI'ER: You came here secretly again?

XU SIX (*takes out a small paper bag from his pocket*): Little Ni'er, you are going to marry Missy Liu. Dad bought two pairs of socks for you. I'll feel less guilty if you trample me underfoot everyday . . .

LITTLE NI'ER (*also feeling sad*): I can't bear to listen to your talk . . .

XU SIX: Father isn't uncaring about you. I see that Spring Happiness feels regrets now, too . . . (*To* Auntie Liu) Auntie Liu, I want to talk with you. I want little Ni'er to come to live with us for a few days . . .

LITTLE NI'ER: For what? I won't go!

XU SIX: Please listen to me. (*To* Auntie Liu) Many educated youths have returned to the city now. If Little Ni'er is still counted as my daughter, she'll be the only child in our family. Then she'll qualify to return to Beijing. I've got all of the permissions from our neighborhood committee. Now I only need one more seal from Small Well Lane's neighborhood committee . . .

LITTLE NI'ER: Stop thinking about that. I won't go to your place, not even for one day. Mom, you'll never agree to this (*angrily leaves and goes into the Lius' house*).

XU SIX: Hey! (*having no alternative*). Kids' tempers! Auntie Liu (*raises the fruit basket*), I, I want to give Little Mrs. a gift, but I, I don't know how to begin . . .

AUNTIE LIU: Xu Six, I, too, have tried hard to find a way to bring them back to the city. But I have other business to handle now. I think you have a good idea. Let's bring Little Ni'er back to the city first. But not one penny to that Little Mrs. . . .

[Wu Qi, *wearing shabby clothes, enters the courtyard.*]

WU QI: Auntie Liu. Oh, isn't this Brother Xu? I haven't seen you for quite a long time.

XU SIX: You are right. I moved out eighteen or nineteen years ago. You are . . .

WU QI (*smiles bitterly*): I came to Beijing to report the injustices suffered by my family.[86] Train stations, Tiantan Park, sidewalks. . . . I make my home wherever I can . . .

AUNTIE LIU (*to* Wu Qi): Older brother. Don't take this personally. These days I am short of money, too. But I have extra grain coupons. I can help a bit. (*Yells toward the house*) Guizhi! Guizhi! Get some grain coupons for your Uncle Wu . . .

WU QI (*hurriedly stops her*): Don't! Auntie Liu, don't. I didn't come today for that . . .

XU SIX: You?

WU QI (*takes out a red wrapper—money is inside—from his pocket*): Auntie Liu, you are going to take in a daughter-in-law, aren't you? Wu Qi, Wu Qi, came to congratulate you on this happy occasion . . . Wu Qi will never forget Auntie . . . (*moved to tears and makes a deep bow*).

AUNTIE LIU (*her eyes turn red*): Older brother. Older brother (*declines the money*). You can't do this. You are in tighter straits than I am! You run around the whole city to make popcorn for others and are bringing up a bunch of children. . . . I'm so upset that I can't give you a hand, and now you . . . (*starts to cry*).

WU QI (*grasps* Auntie Liu's *hand and puts the money into it*): Auntie, Auntie, please don't be sad. . . . It takes time to know a person. Wu Qi is alive today because of the kindness of Auntie and the old neighbors. I can't use gold to buy the long-standing friendship that Small Well Lane has shown me. Auntie, I know you have great troubles now; please don't hide them from me. Brother Liu is in the hospital; our Er Niu was arrested by those . . . Auntie, if you still will not take this money, Wu Qi, Wu Qi, will kneel down in front of you . . .

SHOPKEEPER SHI (*all of a sudden the Shi Family's door bangs open and* Shopkeeper Shi *comes out*): Auntie Liu! Take the money. Take the money. Please take the money. (*Grasps the hands of* Xu Six *and* Wu Qi) Brothers, stay and have dinner with us tonight! These days your Brother Shi has a lot of unspoken words in his heart. I want to get it all out . . .

WU QI: Brother Shi, not today. My children are making popcorn at the entrance of the lane. Next time, next time I must come . . . (*says good-bye and leaves*).

[Xu Six *is pulled into the house by* Shopkeeper Shi. Auntie Liu *stands in the courtyard staring blankly, with the money* Wu Qi *earned by his sweat and tears in her hands.* Little Cao, *holding eighty-year-old* Grandma Teng's *arm, enters.* Grandma Teng *is still in good health, but her eyes have already failed. She has a walking stick in her left hand and a bowl of goldish-yellow millet in her right hand. She hurries to move ahead while calling* Little Six Nine's *name.*]

GRANDMA TENG: Has Six Nine returned?

LITTLE CAO: Please slow down. Don't spill the millet. Grandma Teng, don't be so old-fashioned. This old stuff won't work . . .

GRANDMA TENG (*insists*): How do you know it won't work? Do you mean I don't know as much as you do? The child was traumatized during the Qingming mourning festival.[87] This millet will help him get over the shock. (*Yells*) Six Nine! Six Nine! (*then*) Fengzhen! Fengzhen!!

AUNTIE LIU: Grandma Teng, I am here!

GRANDMA TENG: Where is Six Nine? Third Son Water told me that he saw Six Nine come in . . . (*Yells*) Six Nine! Six Nine!

AUNTIE SHI (*leads* Six Nine *out*): Grandma Teng, Six Nine is here.

LITTLE SIX NINE (*throws himself into* Grandma Teng's *arms*): Great Grandma!

GRANDMA TENG (*caresses* Six Nine's *head with her two hands again and again*): Baby! My dearest baby! Great Grandma's sweetheart, you really returned home . . . (*her hands are shaking*). A motherless poor child! (*doesn't know how to show her deep love, so she sings a folk song while stroking* Six Nine's *head:* "Stroke, stroke my child, no one will scare you. / Stroke, stroke, my child, no one will steal you").

[Little Cao, *with sparkling tears in his eyes, stops in front of* Six Nine. *He squats down and carefully buttons* Six Nine's *jacket with slightly trembling hands.*]

[Grandma Teng *leads* Six Nine *into the Lius' house.*]

LITTLE CAO (*looks around and sees no one else in the courtyard. He grasps* Auntie Liu's *hand and puts a roll of money into it*): Auntie Liu! (*points to his uniform*) I am a policeman. I can't come on Ni'er and Missy Liu's wedding day. Please accept this little gift as a token from my heart, only ten dollars.... Auntie Liu, you must not refuse it.... I'll feel less shame if you accept this money. I can't give a hand in Er Niu's case, so I always feel ashamed in front of the old neighbors ...

AUNTIE LIU: Old Cao, don't say that, please don't say that ...

[*Suddenly* Little Cao *moves close to* Auntie Liu, *whispering in her ear.*]

AUNTIE LIU (*as if thunder crashed above her*): What! Is this true?!

LITTLE CAO (*holds* Auntie Liu's *hands with all his strength*): Auntie Liu. Auntie Liu. You must not take it too hard, you can't ...

[Little Mrs.'s *cough comes out from the inner courtyard.*]

LITTLE CAO: Auntie Liu, I have to go now. Tell me if you need any help (*exits*).

[Little Mrs. *comes out from the inner courtyard. She seems much more experienced and capable now than ten years ago.*]

LITTLE MRS.: Auntie Liu, I heard that Little Six Nine has returned. The neighborhood committee is going to have a meeting here in our compound to criticize and denounce a counterrevolutionary. It will be better to take Six Nine away ...

AUNTIE LIU: A child won't be in the way of your criticism and denunciation of a counterrevolutionary.

LITTLE MRS.: There is a good reason to ask you to take Six Nine away. Now I have told you, and you have heard what I have said. Whether or not you take him away is your decision ...

[*A flatbed tricycle enters Small Well Lane. Third Son Water wipes sweat from his forehead while coming into the courtyard.*]

THIRD SON WATER (*stands in front of the street gate and shouts*): Come here somebody! Give us a hand! (*then turns around toward outside*). Brother, slow down. Slow down. Be sure not to bump the door frame ... (*critically*). Hey! Look at this! If it was two years ago, this bit of work, I'd do it all by myself ... (*walks backwards while guiding*).

[*Follows him,* Wu Qi, *carrying* Liu Jiaxiang *on his back, steps over the threshold with all his might.* Xu Six, Shopkeeper Shi, Little

Ni'er, *and others run out when they hear* Third Son Water's *yelling. With everybody lending a hand, they carry* Liu Jiaxiang *toward the Lius' house. Hearing the noise,* Grandma Teng *appears at the Lius' door.*]

GRANDMA TENG: Who is it? Who are you carrying?

SHOPKEEPER SHI: Third Brother, why did you carry him back?

THIRD SON WATER: The hospital said that they would not perform the operation if we didn't pay a deposit of four hundred dollars. I told them that Liu Jiaxiang is a worker who has health insurance. But the hospital said that Liu Jiaxiang is not covered by workers' insurance. They'll stop his salary, too.

AUNTIE LIU: How can they do that?

GRANDMA TENG: Jiaxiang's wound is festering. He'll be a cripple if we delay the operation . . .

LITTLE MRS. (*neither supercilious nor obsequious*): Here, I'll explain it. The Trolley Bus Factory has asked the neighborhood committee about Liu Jiaxiang's wound. We told them exactly what has happened and didn't embroider. During those mourning days on Tiananmen Square, Liu Jiaxiang didn't miss a day to rush to the square after each meal.[88] He swindled people of Small Well Lane and brought them there. By the way you, Auntie Liu, also brought dumplings to the monument ever since the lunar New Year. To tell you the truth, if his leg hadn't been broken in the earthquake, he would have already been arrested!

AUNTIE LIU: We can't see a doctor because we don't have any money. . . . They even stopped his salary. You just won't let us live!

LITTLE MRS.: The new society won't allow any person to starve to death. You are still making flyswatters, aren't you?

AUNTIE LIU: But your neighborhood committee has canceled my contract for those flyswatters . . .

LITTLE MRS.: Well, you have the contract to sew buttonholes now, don't you?

AUNTIE LIU: You know very well that I don't have good eyesight. Why did you change my job just now . . . ?

[*Suddenly the speakers in the Earthquake Prevention Headquarters start to broadcast a popular revolutionary song, "Going against the Tide."*]

[Big Horse, *a member of the Workers' Militia, holding up a handheld loudspeaker, passes by the street gate.*]

BIG HORSE: Pay attention! All neighborhood groups! Pay attention! All neighborhood groups! The meeting place has been changed to Compound No. 7. The meeting to criticize and denounce a counterrevolutionary will be held in Compound No. 7. All "Facing-the-Sun Compounds"[89] quickly line up people in your compound! Please line up people in your compound!

LITTLE MRS. (*sneering*): Having any trouble? (*Facing* Auntie Liu *but concentrates her gaze on* Wu Qi) How could you then still have extra grain coupons to give those troublemakers who came to Beijing to report their so-called injustices? (*turns around and enters the inner courtyard*).

[Xu Six, *carrying his fruit basket, wants to follow her.*]

WU QI (*blocks his way with his arms*): Elder Brother Xu, must we really suffer at her hands? We must never give in to her.

XU SIX (*softly pushes* Wu Qi's *arms away*): Brother Wu, for my child's sake, I, I have no sense of shame . . . (*goes into the narrow lane*).

[Big Ox *rushes in, panting.*]

BIG OX: Mom! Mom! Grandma Liu, Grandma Liu! I heard that they are going to criticize and denounce my Auntie Er Niu in today's meeting . . .

GRANDMA TENG: What? Who told you that?

BIG OX: All Small Well Lane knows. People are telling each other.

AUNTIE LIU: Grandma Teng, it is true. Little Cao has just . . . told me all . . .

GRANDMA TENG (*bristles with anger*): They knew that Jiaxiang is bedridden. They knew that Missy Liu is getting married. Why must they come here to criticize your own child in front of you? They have no human feelings. They're made of stone.

[*At this moment the Lius' door flies open.* Little Six Nine *stands at the doorway, looking at people like an adult—with a stern expression. His eyes are brimming with tears. Suddenly* Auntie Liu *leans on* Grandma Teng's *shoulder and starts to cry.*]

GRANDMA TENG: Fengzhen! Don't cry. Crying can't solve problems (*but her face, too, is bathed in tears*). Crying can't change their evil hearts! Both my eyes have gone blind from crying too much. . . . Our Jiaxiang, how honest a worker he is. Er Niu wouldn't even step on an ant. Little Six Nine, is only a child but has been scared out of his senses. . . . They are pushing me to the limit . . .

[*Suddenly an old man's choking crying from the Lius' house shakes everyone. It is* Liu Jiaxiang! *This kindhearted and humorous man finally can take no more and cries his heart out.* Auntie Liu *is seized with endless fear. She holds tightly to* Grandma Teng's *arm and starts to shout.*]

AUNTIE LIU: Shiniang![90] Shiniang! I am losing my mind. Soon they'll bring Er Niu here. We must not let Er Niu see Six Nine! Children are mothers' flesh and blood. If Er Niu saw that Six Nine is mentally . . .

GRANDMA TENG (*anxiously*): Third Son Water! Third Son Water! You take Six Nine away from here. Let Six Nine go with us.

THIRD SON WATER (*leads* Six Nine *from the doorway*): Six Nine, you are a good boy. Follow Third Grandpa. Third Grandpa has children's books . . .

LITTLE SIX NINE (*sees tears at the corner of* Third Son Water's *eyes*): Third Grandpa, are you crying?

THIRD SON WATER (*lowers his head*): No. Third Grandpa has never shed one tear in his life . . .

LITTLE SIX NINE: My Grandpa told me that Third Grandpa studied martial arts from Master Teng, and Third Grandpa is an iron man . . .

THIRD SON WATER (*raises his head*): Third Grandpa is an iron man. Six Nine, stay with Third Grandpa. If anyone dares to touch even one of your hairs, Third Grandpa will fight to the last drop of his blood.

GRANDMA TENG: Fengzhen! You don't need to worry about money. I'll collect some for you. To save Jiaxiang's leg, I, I don't care if I lose my pride. Don't laugh at your Shiniang . . .

THIRD SON WATER (*worried*): Mother, what are you going to do? We have a lot of people on our side. We can't let you hurt yourself! If anything untoward should happen to you, Third Son Water . . . (*too upset to continue speaking*).

GRANDMA TENG: What can your mother do? I have decided . . . I have decided to do this. (*Determinedly*) Third Son Water, lead Six Nine and hold my arm. Let's go . . .

[Xu Six, *carrying his fruit basket, lowering his head, comes out from the narrow lane.*]

SHOPKEEPER SHI (*steps forward*): What's going on? She didn't agree?

[Xu Six *shakes his head.* Shopkeeper Shi *snatches the fruit basket and throws it down the hallway.*]

SHOPKEEPER SHI (*gnashing his teeth*): Daughter of a witch. She won't let us live (*with his hands clasped behind his back, paces like a wolf and attempts to figure out a way. His eyes shine when he shoots a glance at* Big Ox). Big Ox. Come here.

[Big Ox *walks over toward him.*]

SHOPKEEPER SHI: Didn't you say that your friends were assigned to a crematorium?

BIG OX (*nods his head*): Yes, I did.

SHOPKEEPER SHI: Can you confide in them?

BIG OX: Of course. We are sworn brothers.

SHOPKEEPER SHI (*catches hold of* Big Ox's *hand*): Come to my house! I have something to talk about with you. (*Pulls* Xu Six *next*) You come, too.

[Shopkeeper Shi, Xu Six, *and* Big Ox *enter the north house.*]

[*Only* Wu Qi, Auntie Liu, Auntie Shi, *and* Auntie Jiu *are left in the courtyard.*]

AUNTIE SHI: Auntie Liu, how about this, we all leave the compound and just lock the street gate. Give them an "empty-city stratagem"[91] . . .

AUNTIE LIU (*shakes her head*): No, no, I want to see my Er Niu.

[*The speaker blares the song "Going against the Tide." Big Horse continues to announce the meeting through his hand-held loudspeaker. The whistling of its feedback and the yells of "Time for the meeting! Time for the meeting!" reverberate through the whole lane.*]

AUNTIE LIU (*grabs* Little Ni'er *and* Auntie Jiu's *hands tightly and hurriedly says*): Children, remember: in front of them, no tears. Do you hear me? (*wipes her eyes thoroughly and takes her stand*).

[Shopkeeper Shi *whispers in* Big Ox's *ear and sends him out of the street gate.* Little Mrs. *hears the whistling sounds and comes out. A policeman,* Big Horse, *and* Little Cao *escort* Er Niu *into the courtyard. The courtyard is quiet.*]

ER NIU (*walks toward* Auntie Liu): Mom!

AUNTIE LIU: Er Niu, if you are my daughter, you must have no tears.

ER NIU: I remember your words. Mother, where is Six Nine?

AUNTIE LIU: Grandma took him away.

ER NIU: How is Grandma?

AUNTIE LIU: She's fine . . .

ER NIU: Mom, you must tell Six Nine that his mother is not a counterrevolutionary. Also, tell him that he shouldn't blame his father. He divorced me because he had to do that . . .

AUNTIE SHI: Er Niu, Er Niu . . . (*with deep feelings*). Take a look, take a look around! Among our old neighbors, no one's eyes are dry. Raise your head. Child, you are not disgraced. You are not disgraced today. The old neighbors in Small Well Lane all know you . . .

[*In the silence a sudden and heartbreaking cry of an old lady pierces the air. It is* Grandma Teng. *She shouts in a hoarse, anxious voice. It is like thunder booming above Small Well Lane.* "My old neighbors!

My old neighbors . . ." Grandma Teng *staggers along groping the street gate. Her silver hair is disheveled and fluttering in the wind. She props herself up by the walking stick in her right hand. In her left hand she carries a bamboo basket. She fumbles ahead with her walking stick and enters the courtyard.]*

[*Everybody in the courtyard is stupefied. The courtyard falls into a dead silence.*]

GRANDMA TENG (*stands in front of the gate*): My old neighbors. My old neighbors in Small Well Lane. Liu Jiaxiang has had his leg crushed. And his daughter was arrested because she went to mourn Prime Minister Zhou. The Liu family, the Liu family has nothing in the pot. My old neighbors. For Grandma Teng's sake, please help the Liu family to pass through their great troubles.

[*People are shaken and dumbstruck. In the dead silence one can only hear sobbing.*]

GRANDMA TENG (*to herself*): Is nobody here? Why does no one answer?

[Er Niu's *mouth is covered harshly by* Auntie Liu *when she is about to cry out "Grandma!"* Auntie Liu *first wipes her eyes and then walks gently toward* Grandma Teng. *She takes out the red envelopes with money inside that* Little Cao *and* Wu Qi *gave her for* Little Ni'er *and* Missy Liu's *wedding and puts them into* Grandma Teng's *basket. She then fishes out several coins that are all she has left from her pocket and spreads them into the basket. In the suffocating silence one hears nothing but the clear and melodious sound of falling coins.*]

GRANDMA TENG: Who are you? Why didn't you say anything? There is no one in Small Well Lane I don't know. Who are you? (*surprised as she strokes the money*). You gave me so much money? (*throwing her walking stick away and gently stroking* Auntie Liu's *head again and again*). Whose mother are you? Good child, may you live for a hundred years. I kowtow to you for Liu Jiaxiang, for Liu Jiaxiang's family, and for our Little Six Nine . . . *(with a thud she kneels down)*.

PEOPLE (*unable to bear it any longer, they cry out*): Grandma Teng!

AUNTIE LIU (*sobs, plaintively*): Shiniang! (*kneels down in front of* Grandma Teng).

GRANDMA TENG (*shocked*): Ah?! You are Fengzhen! (*the bamboo basket in her hand turns over on to the ground*). Fengzhen, don't blame your Shiniang! I know that you feel too shy to talk about your troubles. But I am really worried about Jiaxiang's leg . . .

[Third Son Water *anxiously rushes into the courtyard and hurriedly props up* Grandma Teng.]

THIRD SON WATER: Mother! Mother! Please don't do this. The old neighbors can't stand to see you this way . . .

[Auntie Jiu *picks up the basket.* Shopkeeper Shi, Xu Six, Little Cao, *and even* Big Horse *put money they have into the basket. Little* Liben *also walks forward and puts money into the basket.*]

GRANDMA TENG (*flatly refuses* Third Son Water): Don't bother about me. Auntie Jiu, hold my arm and lead me out.

[Auntie Jiu *is unable to make her change her mind, so she holds* Grandma Teng's *arm, they exit. Again,* Grandma Teng's *grieved cries float in from the street.*]

LITTLE MRS.: We can't hold this meeting now. (*To the policeman*) Please take the prisoner away.

[*At this moment* Little Six Nine *rushes into the courtyard like a madman.*]

LITTLE SIX NINE (*shouts wildly*): Mom! Mom! I am Six Nine (*throws himself toward his mother*).

ER NIU: Six Nine, Momma is here! Momma is here! Let me hold you . . . (*attempts to hold* Six Nine *but can't because she is handcuffed*).

THIRD SON WATER (*stupefied at the beginning, but immediately realizes what he should do. He holds up* Little Six Nine *and walks over to* Er Niu): Kiss your mother. Six Nine. Kiss your mother.

[Little Six Nine *kisses* Er Niu's *face with all his might.*]

LITTLE SIX NINE (*raises the glasses in his hand*): Mom, these are your glasses. You need them to correct students' work (*then he hurriedly whispers in his mother's ear*).

ER NIU (*scared*): Don't. Be a good child. Don't. Listen to Momma, don't do that . . .

POLICEMAN (*with a heavy heart*): Let's go!

LITTLE SIX NINE (*suddenly holds the policeman's arms tightly and cries loudly*): Momma, run. Run away quickly!

[*The policeman doesn't struggle to get rid of* Six Nine; *instead, he watches the child with sympathy.*]

ER NIU: Six Nine. Listen to Momma. Let him go. Wait for Momma . . . sooner or later, Momma will be back.

[Little Six Nine *is confused and lets the policeman go. He throws himself into* Third Son Water's *arms and cries bitterly.*]

POLICEMAN (*still, repeats the words with a heavy heart*): Let's go . . .

[*The policeman escorts* Er Niu *out.* Third Son Water *leads* Little Six Nine *out following them.* Little Mrs. *turns around and attempts to go into the inner courtyard.* Wu Qi *catches up with her in a few steps.*]

WU QI (*points at* Little Mrs.'s *nose*): You! Let's be frank and honest. You drove me away only because you wanted to occupy my house. Right now your nephew still lives there. I'll bring a lawsuit against you. I'll do it as long as I am alive. I'll travel around the whole of Beijing making popcorn, I have a mouth . . .

LITTLE MRS. (*venomously*): I really regret it. At the beginning of the Cultural Revolution, I should have driven you all away.

[*A vehicle horn blows. A strong young man in his twenties, with a filter-tip cigarette tucked behind his ear, steps back while waving his arm to guide the vehicle: "Back up! . . . Back up! Back up! Stop!" The vehicle with blue and white lines on it is a special crematory hearse. The vehicle stops outside of the courtyard, with a screeching of breaks. The fellow who directed the vehicle and the other two broad-shouldered and solidly built young men enter the courtyard.*]

FIRST YOUNG MAN (*takes out a shabby notebook with rolled-up corners from his pocket, turns a few pages of it, then bellows*): Is this Compound No. 7, Small Well Lane?

SHOPKEEPER SHI (*steps forward*): This is No. 7! You are . . .

SECOND YOUNG MAN: Crematorium (*his thumb motions behind him*). The hearse.

FIRST YOUNG MAN (*still lowering his head to read the notebook*): Who is Wang Baode?

LITTLE LIBEN (*feeling puzzled*): I, I am Wang Baode . . .

FIRST YOUNG MAN: Did you call the crematorium?

LITTLE LIBEN: No, I didn't. Nobody in our family died.

FIRST YOUNG MAN: Where is your wife, Zhou Shuying?

LITTLE MRS.: That's me . . .

FIRST YOUNG MAN: It's you? (*looks at her all around*). How can you be standing up again? (*He thumbs toward the hearse.*) Get in!

LITTLE MRS.: Why should I get in? I didn't die!

SECOND YOUNG MAN: No one died? Why did you call the crematorium?

LITTLE LIBEN: Comrades, we truly didn't call you . . .

FIRST YOUNG MAN (*presses on toward* Little Mrs.): You are Zhou Shuying, aren't you? We came to deliver your body. Get in the hearse!

THIRD YOUNG MAN: Don't waste time on her. Who cares whether she's dead or alive—just drag her away.

SECOND YOUNG MAN (*points at* Little Mrs.): I have long heard that you are the local tyrant. Listen: from now on we'll come to drag you away on New Year's Day and every other festival. Brothers, drag her to the hearse.

[*Three young men carry* Little Mrs. *by force to the truck. Little Mrs. shouts and struggles but has no way to get away from these young men.*]

LITTLE LIBEN (*catches up to* Little Mrs.): I owe all my bad luck to you. After all these years I have finally seen through you. You are really nothing. You have offended all the old neighbors. (*Waves her away*) Take her away! Take her away! I don't care! I want a divorce! (*angrily returns to the inner courtyard*).

[*The crematory vehicle exits Small Well Lane with sirens blaring.*]

[*Shopkeeper Shi lights a cigarette and narrows his eyes to watch the hearse slowly leaves the lane. . . . Big Ox is very excited as he runs into the courtyard.*]

BIG OX: Grandpa Shi! Grandpa Shi! (*Secretly*) Did you hear? (*forces himself to cool down and gets close to* Shopkeeper Shi's *ear and whispers*).

[*An expression of unusual excitement appears on* Shopkeeper Shi's *face. The muscles on the corner of his mouth twitch. This must be inspiring news.*]

[Big Ox *whispers in* Third Son Water's *ear. Small Well Lane's old neighbors whisper this great news around one by one.*]

SHOPKEEPER SHI (*his voice is trembling*): Big Ox, what you have told me, is it true?

BIG OX: Of course, it's no lie! Listen!

[*From the distance rises the sounds of firecrackers, gongs and drums, and slogan shouting. These sounds grow louder and louder . . .*][92]

SHOPKEEPER SHI (*sheds tears of happiness and shouts*): Big Ox! Go buy wine for your Grandpa Shi!

[*The Lius' door flies open with a bang. Liu Jiaxiang, dragging his broken leg, leans himself against the door frame. He is laughing, but then his cheeks begin to twitch, and finally he cries out loudly . . .*]

LIU JIAXIANG (*yells while crying*): Third Brother! Third Brother! . . .

THIRD SON WATER, XU SIX, and WU QI (*almost shout at the same time*): Big Ox! Hurry! Buy wine for your grandpa!

[*A deafening sound of gongs and drums and firecrackers resounds through the skies. The people in No. 7 compound are immersed in wild happiness after they have been through a bitterly long journey at sea and finally returned to solid ground again.*]

(CURTAIN)

ACT FIVE

TIME Summer 1980. Sunset. Three days after the reelection of the Small Well Lane neighborhood committee.

PLACE Small Well Lane.

SCENE The sun casts an orange glow upon Small Well Lane. It has been a hot day, and the air is just cooling down. After dinner the hardworking people pour cold water on the street, making the lane cool and refreshing. People who have had a busy day now carry folding chairs and stools out one after another, sitting in the shade of the tree, chatting and relaxing. From appearances they seem as quiet and peaceful as usual, but, in fact, all of them are worried about the reelection results . . .

The lane looks much more aesthetically pleasing than it did in act IV. An asphalt road has replaced the old dirt track full of bumps and hollows. All the courtyard walls and arches ruined in the earthquake have been fixed. The lane looks very neat but also seems narrower than before. Most families don't have space for those educated youth who now have returned to the city from the countryside.[93] Thus, extra rooms have been built in front or behind main houses.

Popular music performed by electric guitar and *pi-pa*[94] floats in from the south entrance. The fashionable Western instrument does not seem to fit with the traditional Chinese instrument. Still, the music is happy and relaxed, so no one feels uncomfortable, even though the instruments don't go together well. The north entrance, which was once a small market during the early years, is now a newly opened free market.[95] The distant buzzing sounds come from there.

Farmers carrying bags on their backs, scales in their hands, and eggs in their baskets occasionally pass by the lane while calling out their wares. One can feel a relaxed but tired atmosphere through the whole lane after many years of bitter struggle.

> [CURTAIN RISES. *Under the streetlight* Third Son Water *and* Big Ox *are playing Chinese chess intently.* Shopkeeper Shi, *holding a transistor radio with two hands, lies on a folded deck chair. He narrows his eyes as he enjoys a rendition of* Yue Fei.[96] *The current chapter is:* "*The Qingui couple plot murder at the eastern window, Yue Fei and his son's souls return to Heaven at Wind and Wave Pavilion.*" Liu Jiaxiang,*wearing a pair of slippers, carrying a newspaper under his arm, with a folded stool in his left hand and a teacup in his right hand, strolls out the street gate. The radio stops broadcasting* Yue Fei.]

SHOPKEEPER SHI (*turns off the radio and opens his eyes to look around; at first glance he catches* Liu Jiaxiang): Brother Liu! Brother Liu (*raises himself to a half-sitting position*), you know, no matter how great a hero he was, he couldn't put his ability to good use when those treacherous court officials were in power. (*Points to his radio*) Listening to the story, my heart feels heavy ...

LIU JIAXIANG (*sitting on his folding stool*): That goes without saying. Whenever treacherous court officials are in power, good people have no peace. I'm not talking about a huge country but just our Small Well Lane (*holds up his little finger*). Once she rose to power ... during the years the Gang of Four were in power, did we suffer!

SHOPKEEPER SHI: Brother Liu, tell you the truth, I want to write to our government! I'll ask them to figure out a way and to make a law that guarantees that capable people can put their abilities to good use. China has a lot of able people ...

LIU JIAXIANG: We need to change the regulations (*holds up* Reference News).[97] Read the news in this newspaper. The chief minister of the Petroleum Ministry was fired.

> [Wu Qi, *carrying two pounds of fresh noodles in his right hand, scratching his back with a back scratcher in his left hand, enters from the south end of the lane.*]

A prosperous alley in early spring.

WU QI (*continues for* Liu): Good thing to fire him. This time don't you think that the higher-ups have really made up their minds. Otherwise, they wouldn't ask us to reelect the neighborhood committee ...

SHOPKEEPER SHI: Brother Wu, take a seat. I'd like to have a heart-to-heart talk with my friends (*moves closer to* Wu Qi *and lowers his voice*). I feel unsure. This time (*holds up his little finger*) do you think she really will be dismissed as head of the neighborhood committee?

LIU JIAXIANG (*unconcerned*): You worry too much. Why do you feel unsure? People didn't elect her. Is the election just a game? Is it only to amuse our old neighbors? Then it wouldn't be democracy.

SHOPKEEPER SHI (*his head shakes like a rattle drum*): Brother Liu, let me cut in. This matter is still not certain. Three days already, why hasn't it been approved? I'll tell you another fact: if Old Cao hadn't shown up for the election himself, the election would have vanished like soap bubbles, and Auntie Liu could never be elected. Brother Wu, am I right?

WU QI: I won't feel sure until the new neighborhood committee is approved. We should hurry up and change the old regulations. I'm more than ready for this change. We common folk have already suffered so many years; finally, we have hope again.

[*Just then the talking is punctuated by the quarrel between* Third Son Water *and* Big Ox *at the chessboard.*]

THIRD SON WATER: Are you moving your chessman?! Put it there. Stinking lump of shit ...

BIG OX (*grinning cheekily*): Third Grandpa, let me change one step, only one move. It's said that to take the chariot you must declare but take the horse quietly and eat the cannon secretly. You got my chariot.

THIRD SON WATER (*laughing*): You child! (*puts down the chessman and walks over*). Wu Qi, don't let this worry you all the time. The Gang of Four are a thing of the past. Little Mrs., she can't cause trouble anymore. Isn't there a meeting at seven o'clock tonight? We'll know the results when Old Cao comes.

[Little Ring, *using his two hands to carry a scale with mutton inside, comes from the free market.*]

LITTLE RING (*walks over to* Third Son Water): Third Uncle, this is the leftover I kept for you. Can you see that big chop, little chop, or ribs. . . . For hot pot mutton nothing tastes better than this! I have cut you a full plate of meat . . .

SHOPKEEPER SHI: We should wait until fall to eat hot pot mutton. Hot pot mutton in summer tastes just like cotton—you only get the gravy . . .

THIRD SON WATER (*intentionally threatening*): Little Ring, you have been very busy recently. Listen to me, take it easy. Who knows, one day they may again pull the capitalist tails . . .[98]

LITTLE RING (*distinguishes political winds better than anyone else in No. 7 compound*): You shouldn't joke about such things. Political policy is difficult to guess, changes in a minute. I'll stop business as soon as I see a change. Do you hear that? (*holds up his little finger*). She has been removed from her post, but! Old Cao, Old Cao will be transferred to another post too. He'll be banished to Heaven River to be in charge of prisoners . . .

PEOPLE (*shocked to learn that*): Ah? Is this true?

LITTLE RING: Believe it or not! For the past six months Little Ring hasn't told one lie.

LIU JIAXIANG: She, she has such power? She can really remove Old Cao from his post?

[*Suddenly* Shopkeeper Shi *coughs hard. Everybody stops talking.* Little Mrs. *leads a hick pear peddler in from the south end. The pear peddler carries a cloth bag on his shoulder and is overwhelmed with joy.*]

LITTLE MRS. (*very intimately*): . . . You don't need a note from me, just tell him that it's me who sent you there. He'll certainly arrange your lodging (*points ahead with her finger*). Cross the street, only a few blocks from the place where you were selling pears. Remember, it is called "Small Bridge Motel."

PEAR PEDDLER: . . . Elder Niece, I know that my pears are not good enough. You may reduce the price if . . .

LITTLE MRS.: Second Uncle, I can help you sell them all without cutting one penny of the price! I've already talked to the neighbors . . .

[*When she raises her head, she sees* Third Son Water *and the others. She looks a bit nervous and quickly lowers her head and leaves.*]

WU QI: See! She is still that cocky. Bringing some damn pears to the lane and hawking them. Who dares not to go to buy them? Who dares? I remember collecting subscriptions for Commissioner Ding—Big Shot in those old days . . .

LITTLE RING: Did you see that? She doesn't look like she's in trouble. See you later (*exits*).

LIU JIAXIANG: Damn! Is this fellow telling the truth?

THIRD SON WATER: Don't believe him. Little Ring, he's the master of bullshit. You shouldn't listen to him. Did you see that she didn't dare face me eye to eye? Her spirit is flagging. She can't budge Old Cao.

[*Everybody still feels uncertain.* Auntie Liu *and* Auntie Jiu *are carrying a desk with two drawers out from the compound.*]

THIRD SON WATER (*having fun*): What's this? Will the new head of the neighborhood committee open court today?

BIG OX (*shouting*): Court is in session.

AUNTIE JIU (*giving* Big Ox *a slap on his back*): Don't be rude to an elder! Get out of here!

[Big Ox *pulls* Third Son Water *over to finish playing chess.*]

WU QI: Auntie Liu, when will you start to handle neighborhood business? I'll be the first one to file a lawsuit. I have my residence permit but still haven't gotten my house back. Little Mrs.'s nephew has moved out, but she herself moved in . . .

AUNTIE LIU: My office is smaller than a cabbage seed. Elder brother, I truly fear . . .

LIU JIAXIANG (*doesn't like hearing this*): Here you go again!

AUNTIE LIU: Don't tease me. Little Mrs. has her connections at every level.

LIU JIAXIANG (*interrupts*): Connections. Has powerful connections. It's no longer the time of the Gang of Four. (*His concern about Old Cao's job transfer makes him really angry.*) Today is my birthday, why must you make me unhappy?

AUNTIE LIU: I didn't say I won't take this position. All right, you are the master . . .

WU QI: Auntie, you must not show your confusion. Yesterday Xu Six told me that Little Mrs. visited Spring Happiness and tricked her into taking Little Ni'er back . . .

[Auntie Shi *carries a bamboo basket out and attempts to slip away behind* Shopkeeper Shi.]

SHOPKEEPER SHI (*noticing* Auntie Shi): Where are you going? You!

AUNTIE SHI (*knows that she is in the wrong, stops*): The head of the neighborhood committee's uncle has brought some pears here that didn't sell out in the market . . .

LIU JIAXIANG: You call those pears? They look like jujube cherries, but still they sell for thirty cents a pound.

WU QI: Auntie Shi, you are really still under her control. Why are you so scared of her?

AUNTIE SHI: It's not like that. Brother Wu, please don't be angry at me. We can afford to buy a TV; why should we worry about a few cents? I prefer to spend money rather than being upset . . .

LIU JIAXIANG: You, you, must have heard that the election hasn't been approved. So you feel diffident. (*Embarrassing her*) Up to today, I have never seen Brother Shi afraid of anyone.

SHOPKEEPER SHI: Get back. If you buy those pears today, I'll smash the TV.

AUNTIE JIU: Auntie Shi (*holds up her little finger*), she has been driven out of office. Why do you still feel uncertain? (*sighs with emotion*). For so many years my heart has always been stuck in my throat. Each New Year or holiday she brought people to our house to check our residence cards! She knew that she couldn't find anything wrong. She did it on purpose just to embarrass us . . .

AUNTIE SHI: You all know nothing. Old Cao. . . . Hey.

[Chen Jiuling, *wearing a horrible yellowish shirt and pants, enters. He doesn't look old, though more than ten years has passed. He only looks darker.*]

CHEN JIULING (*pats* Big Ox's *shoulder*): Comrade, I'd like to ask you about someone—does Big Ox's family still live here?

BIG OX (*doesn't raise his head*): Don't call Big Ox "Big Ox"! Who are you?

CHEN JIULING: I am his father!

BIG OX (*rises*): You are his father? I am Big Ox! Big Ox doesn't have such a country bumpkin father. Bug off!

CHEN JIULING: What! You complain of your shabby dad. Damn, children never mind how bad-looking their mothers are; dogs never care about how poor their master's household is . . .

SHOPKEEPER SHI: Little Jiu? Are you Little Jiu?

CHEN JIULING: You are . . . (*recognizes him at once*). Uncle! Uncle! I've missed you so much . . . (*cries*).

SHOPKEEPER SHI: This time, you were not thrown back by the rebels?

[Big Ox *turns and hurries to* Auntie Jiu.]

CHEN JIULING (*blows his nose before continuing; he still loves talking*): Uncle! Auntie! Fifteen years. Fifteen years to the day. Guess where they took me to? Xinjiang.[99] Go west from Xinjiang! Hey, the head of our labor team is a big guy with a hot temper. But remember that Chen Jiuling is always a great fellow, no matter where he is. Grow vegetables? The vegetables froze there. Did Chen Jiuling fail to grow them? No way (*speaking with the help of gestures*). When the sun went down, I made little walls of mud to protect each and every tiny sprout from the cold. . . . The day I left the labor team, our team head, that big man, shed tears . . .

AUNTIE JIU: You, you half-wit! (*pulls him into the courtyard*).

CHEN JIULING: Hey! Hey? Oh! You are Big Ox's mother.

[Chen Jiuling, Auntie Jiu, *and* Big Ox *enter the courtyard. People, one after another, follow them in.* Spring Happiness, *carrying a cookie box, follows* Xu Six *in from the north entrance. When she sees the old neighbors, she stops.*]

XU SIX: ... Come on! Haven't we made up our minds?

AUNTIE SHI: Are you? Spring Happiness! (*forgets the old grudge between them as she shouts toward the courtyard*). Auntie Liu! Auntie Liu! Spring Happiness is here! Spring Happiness is here!

LIU JIAXIANG: Spring Happiness! You, you, my in-law, how did you find the time to come?

[Auntie Liu, Auntie Jiu, *and* Little Ni'er *hearing the news come out.*]

SPRING HAPPINESS: ... I came to visit the old neighbors. ... Auntie Liu, I shouldn't do that in the first place. ... I miss our Little Ni'er. ... I cannot stand it anymore ... (*tears in her eyes*).

AUNTIE LIU (*holds* Spring Happiness's *hands*): Spring Happiness, this is Little Ni'er! She and Missy Liu have both returned to the city! Little Ni'er, come here! Say hello to her! (*Orders*) Say hello to your mother!

[Little Ni'er *lowers her head, saying nothing.*]

SPRING HAPPINESS: Little Ni'er, good girl, mother begs your forgiveness. For so many years I have wanted to come, but I felt too ashamed. Today, in front of the old neighbors, if you could call me once, call me mother once, I would close my eyes and die without regret ...

LITTLE NI'ER: ... Mother!

SPRING HAPPINESS: Eh, my good girl. Xu Six, we can go now.

LIU JIAXIANG: Auntie Liu (*blocks* Xu Six *and* Spring Happiness's *way*). No, no, Don't leave! Having come so far, how can you leave right away?

AUNTIE SHI: Spring Happiness, please don't go. I am the one with a sharp mouth but a soft heart. I feel so sad when I hear Little Ni'er calling you mother. We were old neighbors—why should we keep fighting? It's my fault ...

SPRING HAPPINESS: Auntie Shi! Who knows whose fault it is. It seems I have been living in a bad dream all these years. I feel exhausted, deadly exhausted, and dull. ... Auntie Liu, have you heard? The day before yesterday, Little Mrs. unexpectedly came to my house and told me: "The Liu Family has both a grown-up daughter and a son. They have no reason to keep Little Ni'er. You should sue them!"

SHOPKEEPER SHI: Auntie Six,[100] don't let yourself be fooled. She's just trying to stir you up against the Lius.

SPRING HAPPINESS: Elder Brother Shi, you needn't remind me, I know it well. Isn't she a despicable creature? A political climber.

LIU JIAXIANG: My dear in-law, come inside. Come inside and let's chat . . .

[Er Niu *comes from the south entrance with a newspaper in her hand.*]

ER NIU (*sees* Wu Qi *at first glance*): Uncle Wu, Auntie Wu is cursing you in front of your house: "The old good-for-nothing! Here I am waiting for noodles to cook; he must have gone somewhere to yak again."

WU QI (*hurriedly takes the noodles from the stool*): Oh, the freshly made noodles are all dried up! I forgot them . . . (*exits hurriedly*).

SHOPKEEPER SHI: Where is Six Nine?

ER NIU: His grandma took him away . . .

AUNTIE SHI: Er Niu, you should remarry now and settle this whole business. He's a man, and he's already come a half-dozen times to apologize. You should accept him.

ER NIU: I'm not in a hurry. Why must you worry? I'll keep up these airs another two days, and then it will be the fourth anniversary of our divorce. Understand? (*holds up the newspaper in her hand*). I almost forgot this important news! Papa, the newspaper has an article about our Small Well Lane's election.

[*Everybody in the courtyard gathers around* Er Niu.]

LIU JIAXIANG: Is it true? What did they say in the newspaper? Read it!

ER NIU: The newspaper says that the old Small Well Lane neighborhood committee was a false model. . . . The newspaper says that the committee was responsible for the death of Ma Deqing, Uncle Ma. The newspaper also points out that Chen Jiuling was thrown back by the rebels, but the committee wrote to the supervisory office and said that Chen Jiuling escaped from jail and returned to Small Well Lane to sabotage Small Well Lane's Cultural Revolution . . . (*her finger moves quickly across the newspaper*). Here, here, it mentions Uncle Wu's house. The newspaper says that almost all the members in the old neighborhood committee had occupied the other residents' nicer homes during the turmoil . . .

SHOPKEEPER SHI: Great! This is a great article!

ER NIU: Listen to this paragraph (*reads*): "The democratically elected Small Well Lane Neighborhood Committee that has been expected for so long is finally here. But the new neighborhood committee still hasn't been approved by the relevant authorities. Small Well Lane residents are anxiously waiting for . . ."

LIU JIAXIANG: Who wrote this article?

ER NIU: There are two names: one is called Ma Baoguo; the other is called Xiao Liben. (*Lowering her voice*) Someone told me that Xiao Liben is Little Liben.

PEOPLE: Really?

ER NIU: Listen to the pronunciation of these two names: Xiao Liben and Xiao (Little) Liben.

AUNTIE SHI: Who is that Ma what's-his-name? It sounds familiar . . .

SHOPKEEPER SHI: Ma Baoguo? (*Suddenly recalls*) Oh! It must be Qishi'er, Ma Deqing's son!

LIU JIAXIANG: Can it be him?

SHOPKEEPER SHI: Must be him. He went back to the newspaper to be a reporter after being rehabilitated. It's him.

LIU JIAXIANG: Ah! I remember, too. People said that it was he who went to Compound No. 5 to hold several forums there a few days ago (*sighs with emotion*). What a guy. He was exiled for so many years, but he's still honest and frank . . .

ER NIU: Father, people on the street are all saying that Old Cao is going to be transferred. Is that true?

[*Everyone suddenly feels upset, and nobody wants to continue the topic. In the silence the radio begins the "pips" to record the hour: it's seven o'-clock. Also,* Wu Qi's *call "It's time for the meeting! It's time for the meeting!" can be heard from a distance. People carrying small folded stools come to listen to the election results.* Wu Qi *rushes in with full of joy.*]

WU QI: Old Cao is coming! Old Cao is coming! Old Cao is going to be transferred, but he isn't being discharged from his office. He's been promoted! He'll be a section chief in the Public Security Bureau (*all of a sudden he bursts out crying*).

PEOPLE (*in happy astonishment*): Really?

THIRD SON WATER: What have I said? Good people will finally get good fortune.

[Little Cao, *with a cookie box in his hand, comes from the north entrance. He feels profoundly reluctant to part with Small Well Lane's old neighbors.*]

SHOPKEEPER SHI, THIRD SON WATER, LIU JIAXIANG, and WU QI: Old Cao! Old Cao! Is that true? You'll be promoted to a higher position in the bureau?

LITTLE CAO: Third Uncle, Uncle Shi, I am coming to say good-bye to my old neighbors... (*gazes with deep feeling at* Small Well Lane *and the people he has been working together with every day from morning to night*). When I started to work in Small Well Lane, everyone here called me Little Cao. I was only this tall! Every auntie darned socks and cleaned cotton-padded jackets for me. Grandma Teng treats me as her own grandson. Whenever she had a little bit of food, she would leave some for me. But what have I, Little Cao, done for my neighbors... (*on the verge of tears*)?

AUNTIE LIU: Old Cao, don't go on like this.

LITTLE CAO: I've been working here for more than twenty years. The longer I worked together with you, the closer I became with my old neighbors. Where can I find people like those of Small Well Lane? You are so good, so kind (*moved to tears*).

[*The old neighbors join him in shedding tears.*]

LIU JIAXIANG: Old Cao, we all know the kind of person you are. It's wonderful that you have been promoted. This is a joyous occasion. The Small Well Lane is still in your district, isn't it? Our old neighbors hate to part with you, but we are happy to see you moving ahead.

PEOPLE: Right!

LITTLE CAO (*smiles through tears*): Yes, let's celebrate the happy event. The leadership has responded to our election of the neighborhood committee! (*Raising his voice*) They support our democratic election. From today on Auntie Liu is the head of Small Well Lane's Neighborhood Committee.

[*People warmly applaud.*]

AUNTIE LIU: Old Cao, Auntie had thought to rely on your help . . .

LITTLE CAO: Rely on the people's help. Rely on the old neighbors' support. Auntie Liu, haven't you seen that?! Never mind the whole country, even in our Small Well, such a small lane, it has been so hard to move ahead. Each step is not easy.

WU QI: Auntie! You have been the head of the neighborhood committee before. You must not be hesitant to take this position. Take it!

SHOPKEEPER SHI: Auntie Liu, take this job. We'll support you.

AUNTIE LIU: I'll take it, for the old neighbors' sake, I'll do it!

LITTLE CAO: My old neighbors, uncles, aunties, good-bye . . . I'll come back to visit you (*holds up the cookie box*). Now I need to go to see Grandma Teng . . .

AUNTIE JIU (*sees* Grandma Teng *coming*): Old Cao, look. Grandma Teng is here. Grandma Teng has come to see you.

[Grandma Teng, *a veritable historical monument for Small Well Lane, is still going strong even though her eyes have failed. She holds a walking stick and comes at a great pace.*]

GRANDMA TENG (*anxiously*): Fengzhen! Fengzhen! Do they say that Little Cao is going to leave? Where is Little Cao? My Cao! Little Cao! (*throws the walking stick away and gropes her way*).

LITTLE CAO (*hurries to greet her*): Grandma Teng, Grandma Teng, here I am. Here I am.

GRANDMA TENG: Little Cao, my good boy, it pains Grandma to see you leave.

[*The square becomes quiet; only the classical music performed by electric guitar and* pi-pa *pounds people's hearts.*]

GRANDMA TENG (*raises her head*): My child, you are a chief officer now. But don't forget your grandma; don't forget Small Well Lane's old neighbors.

LITTLE CAO: Grandma, don't worry, I won't.

GRANDMA TENG: This is our old Beijinger's custom: farewell dumplings and welcome noodles. Fengzhen, we two, mother and daughter, will make dumplings for Little Cao (*takes out a small paper bag from her jacket with a trembling hand*). Here is some Chinese medicine for you. You catch cold so easily. Take them.

LITTLE CAO (*accepts and treasures them*): Grandma, yesterday when I reported for duty at the bureau, the head there asked me to send his greetings to you. He said that he'll come to see you when he has time . . .

GRANDMA TENG: I know. Everybody wants to take a look at our Small Well Lane . . .

[*The electrical guitar and* pi-pa *play loudly.* Grandma Teng *turns around, seems to have regained her sight, and can see everything in front of her. She looks at Small Well Lane and looks at every bush and tree. . . .* Grandma Teng's *silver hair is fluttering in the wind and touching* Little Cao's *face softly, telling him the deepest feelings of Small Well Lane's neighbors, which warm the depths of* Little Cao's *heart . . .*]

LITTLE CAO: Grandma, what are you thinking about?

GRANDMA TENG: My eyes have failed. I can't see what Small Well Lane looks like these days! What do regular folks want now? They only want to live, to live a quiet and stable life in Small Well Lane . . .

[*The distant duet of electric guitar and* pi-pa *grows louder. This time the* pi-pa *takes the lead, and the electric guitar accompanies it. The melody is harmonious, deep, and touching . . .*]

THE END

NOTES

This text is translated from Li Longyun, "Xiaojing hutong" (Small Well Lane), published in *Juben* (Drama), no. 5 (1981): 36–76.

1. Characters in this list are given in the order presented in the Chinese edition. Minor characters, such as Waiter and Pear Peddler, have not been listed here.
2. *Wuxu* year in the old calendar corresponds to 1898 and gives the name to the famous "Wuxu reforms" of that year (also known as the Hundred Days Reform). The author clearly means for Grandma Teng to represent the urges of that first effort at modern, constitutional reform.
3. Translated as Xiao Jieshi, a name indicating the adoptive parents' hope that this frail child would grow up to be a sturdy man.
4. Literally "seventieth son." The Wei Family was rich enough to buy children as "house servants."
5. Traditionally, working-class Chinese would give their children animal nicknames—for example, Big Ox (*Da Niu*)—to help ensure they would grow up strong. *Class of '70* (*qi ling jie*) is a euphemism for coming of age in the middle period of the Cultural Revolution, distinguishing Big Ox from older Red Guards active in the most violent three years of 1966–68, who are known as *lao san jie* (old graduates of the three years).
6. The *gongren minbing* were the paramilitary force used in the mid-1970s by Jiang Qing's faction (later known as the Gang of Four).
7. On the eve of the lunar New Year, one of the most important of the traditional Chinese folk holidays, people were supposed to send the kitchen god to Heaven by burning his image along with proper culinary sacrifices to please him so he would speak well of their families to the bureaucrats in Heaven. The troubled times in this scene contrast with the festive imagery of the holiday.
8. Literally "Northern Peace," the name of the city from 1927 until October 1949, when it became, again, the capital (*jing*), Beijing.
9. Translated as *Niang-niang miao*, the temple of the Bodhisattva, who is in charge of fertility and posterity.
10. A big tree that grows freely in northern China.
11. The Eighth Route Army was the military wing of the CCP during the War of Resistance against Japan. After 1947 it became part of the People's Liberation Army; but people, like those living in Small Well Lane, were slow to adopt the new name.
12. Famous Imperial Shrine in central Beijing that has a large open field around it.
13. Fu Zuoyi was a top nationalist general who surrendered Beiping peacefully to the CCP in 1949. He later served in the government of the People's Republic of China.
14. Translated as *wei maozi*, standing for Tianjin. Yangliuqing was a famous place for making New Year's pictures.

15. A superstitious act, since girls were considered to be less valuable than boys. Auntie Liu's idea was to fool the spirits into thinking her son was a girl so they would not bother with the child.

16. That is, to collect gifts from invited guests to honor the old mother.

17. *Juntong* literally means the "military police," but it was run under the infamous Kuomintang (KMT) spy chief, Dai Li.

18. *Kang* is a raised bed platform in northern Chinese households that is warmed by the flue from the kitchen stove.

19. *Renfanzi* refers to the business of procuring young boys who were castrated and placed into service guarding the Imperial harem during Qing times (1644–1911). By the 1940s it had turned to procuring young girls for the brothels.

20. Literally thirty-six *bai* (obeisance), which serve as the ceremony of adoption, in this case adopting Grandma Teng as Commissioner Ding's mother.

21. People call the wife of one's martial arts teacher, or master, *shiniang* (literally "teacher's mother").

22. Children's laughing indicates that he is unable to see things clearly because his eyes are defective.

23. Jingde zhen is the home of Chinese porcelain manufacture, famous for "Chinaware" inside and outside of China since the Ming Dynasty.

24. Literally "Blessed by the Sangha."

25. Reference unclear. By context Tangen'er must be a place where Qishi'er fears he will be killed.

26. Deng Baoshan and Zang Dongsun were representatives of General Fu Zuoyi, who was the chief commander of the KMT Military in Beiping (named Beijing after 1949), in 1948 to hold talks with CCP Liberation Army for liberating Beiping in peace.

27. These are cherry-sized fruits sugar glazed on a stick, a popular Beijing street snack for children.

28. The red armband signifies that Little Liben is an underground Communist activist.

29. The Great Leap Forward (1958–60) was the grand and tragic development program led by Mao Zedong. It became a disaster because almost everyone joined in the unrealistic plans. For a sense of the elite politics that led to the madness, see Roderick MacFarquhar, *Origins of the Cultural Revolution*, vol. 2: *The Great Leap Forward, 1958–1960* (Oxford: Oxford University Press, 1983); a cinemagraphic account of a similar street during Great Leap Forward is given in Zhang Yimo's recent film *Huozhe* (To Live), which is available on video with English subtitles.

30. See "Sense of Place" in the Introduction for further descriptions of traditional family compounds and alleys with photographs.

31. October 1 is the National Day of the People's Republic of China since 1949.

32. White is an inauspicious color, both in folk traditions, as the color of death, and in the Communist movement, as the color attributed to the CCP's

arch rival, the KMT. Rectification movements are conducted by the CCP to mobilize its constituency. They combine personal self-criticism and the study of policy documents. Properly done, it produces an effective team unified by shared ideology. The classic study of this *zhengfeng* is Frederick C. Teiwes, *Politics and Purges in China: Rectification and the Decline of Party Norms, 1950–1965*, 2d ed. (Armonk, N.Y.: M. E. Sharpe, 1993). Small group study within the rectification process, such as this scene characterizes, is covered in Martin King Whyte, *Small Groups and Political Ritual in China* (Berkeley: University of California Press, 1974).

33. The name for the Chinese volunteer forces that fought against the Americans and the South Koreans in the Korean War (1950–53).

34. The fountain pen is a symbol of higher education and intellectual status, not entirely deserved by this character.

35. These are the ambitious construction projects of the Great Leap Forward, including the National People's Congress and National Museum on Tiananmen Square in Beijing, among other major public buildings. The backyard steel furnaces were a massive disaster promoted by Mao. This mania for reckless economic experimentation at the elite level and the inability of lower-level officials and citizens to resist it is well captured in MacFarquhar, *Origins*, vol. 2; and Zhang Yimou's film *Huozhe*.

36. This is a common expression of supreme devotion to one's parents, as told in the play (*Classic of Filial Piety*). A son in a poor family fed his aged parents by cooking a soup made of pieces of his own flesh.

37. Sanfan, the movement against three evils, ran from 1951 through 1952 and focused on corruption, waste, and bureaucracy. Wufan, the movement against five evils begun in 1952, was directed against bribery, tax evasion, theft of state property, cheating on government contracts, and stealing of economic information. The anti-spy movement, running from 1950 through 1952, was a search for KMT spies during the Korean War. There were in fact spies but not as many as the CCP "found." An excellent account of these political movements is given in A. Doak Barnett, *Communist China: The Early Years, 1949–1955* (New York: Praeger, 1965).

38. The red scarf indicates she is in the Communist Young Pioneers (CYP). Most Chinese children at this time joined the CYP when they reach the age of nine.

39. This refers to another mass campaign during the Great Leap Forward aimed to eradicate the "Four Pests"—rats, sparrows, flies, and mosquitoes.

40. Meaning an honorably discharged war veteran. This phrase echoes the title of a popular post-Mao period essay, "Zui ke'ai de ren" (The most honorable man) by Wei Wei.

41. He is referring to the new People's Communes (*renmin gongshe*), which were pioneered in Henan in 1958. The mention here of Hunan province is a bit odd. It probably serves as a dig at Hua Guofeng—successor to Mao Zedong as Party leader in 1976. The radical Hua had been the leader of Hunan during the Great Leap and, as far as this play is concerned, had been comfortably deposed

from leadership in 1981, the year this play was published. "Satellite" was used during the Leap as a metaphor for the success of *Sputnik,* the Soviet satellite that "beat" the West's into orbit. See MacFarquhar, *Origins,* vol. 2.

42. A unit of area equal to one-sixth of an acre. This much grain from such a small area of land is obviously unrealistic, but people at the time seemed to feel the need to believe it. This issue is discussed in our introduction.

43. Proof of extermination of rats in the Four Pests campaign during the Great Leap Forward.

44. Referring to the May 1957 explosion of intellectual criticism of the CCP in the Hundred Flowers movement. This was followed immediately by the brutal crackdown on those critics in the anti-rightist movement.

45. Grain rationing was universal in urban China from the late 1950s. Urban residents could not buy grain without these coupons, which were distributed to "legal residents" by local Party officials such as Little Cao. People could not move residences freely because only "legal" residents could obtain grain, oil, cloth, and other coupons. The significance of the residence and rationing systems in China is laid out in Tiejun Cheng and Mark Selden, "The Construction of Spatial Hierarchies: China's Hukou and Danwei Systems," in *New Perspectives on State Socialism in China,* ed. Timothy Cheek and Tony Saich (Armonk, N.Y.: M. E. Sharpe, 1997).

46. A common saying, roughly translated as "If you can't rely on your own children, how can you rely on a stepchild?"

47. A polite way to refer to Spring Happiness.

48. She is bemoaning her inability to attract Little Ni'er into her own family.

49. A game played with folded paper triangles—Scarred Squint had made them out of cigarette packages in act 1—similar to tiddlywinks.

50. Referring to the Hundred Flowers movement; see note 41.

51. In northern Manchuria. This is a punishment that the author of this play also suffered; see our introduction.

52. Little Cao is mouthing the ideal attitude of the Communist Party cadre in order to encourage Little Mrs. to tell him who has been criticizing him.

53. The Public Security Office is charged with investigating espionage and political cases, similar to the KGB in Russia or the FBI in the United States. The list here refers to files from the 1940s puppet government of Beiping, which collaborated with the Japanese.

54. These are all fabulous goals of the Great Leap, though public, free dining halls did operate in many areas for a short while.

55. Weather is typically used as a metaphor for political "winds." Here *hot wind* refers to the leftist "heat" of the Cultural Revolution, which had sprung up "out of nowhere" in May 1966.

56. Literally *chuanlian,* "to exchange revolutionary experiences." Red Guards were high school and university student activists encouraged by Mao Zedong to "make revolution" by rebelling against all authorities. In particular,

Red Guards headed Mao's call to support the Cultural Revolution by "exchanging revolutionary experiences" as they traveled to Beijing to join mass rallies in Tiananmen Square. A good example of this lifestyle is given in the account of a former Red Guard, Rae Yang, *The Spider Eaters* (Berkeley: University of California Press, 1996). The best documentary history is Michael Schoenhals, *Not a Dinner Party: The Chinese Cultural Revolution* (Armonk, N.Y.: M. E. Sharpe, 1996). A good political narrative by Chinese scholars is Yan Jiaqi and Gao Gao, *Turbulent Decade: A History of the Cultural Revolution*, ed. D. W. Y. Kwok (Honolulu: University of Hawaii Press, 1996).

57. During the Cultural Revolution Mao's quotations were often set to local musical tunes to increase their popularity among the masses. The Red Guard propaganda studio refers to its broadcasting as a "struggle"—a constant theme during these years.

58. Translated as *yin yang tou*, or "ying yang heads." This was a public humiliation inflicted by the Red Guards in which half of the victim's head was shaved clean.

59. The "Sixteen Articles" was a major policy document of the Cultural Revolution according to which the Red Guards launched their attacks on what they perceived to be antisocialist things. See Michael Schoenhals, *China's Cultural Revolution, 1966–1969: Not a Dinner Party* (New York: M. E. Sharpe, 1996), 65.

60. A sign of bad luck.

61. Matched halves of a poem in the traditional style that are put on either side of the compound door. See the scene description for act 1.

62. The *da zi bao*, "Big Character Poster," was the standard form of public expression during the Cultural Revolution—large sheets of paper with declarations (and usually political denunciations) handwritten by Red Guards, the "masses," or individuals just trying to protect themselves.

63. To "draw a line" was to make a public statement separating oneself from some negative person or idea. Spouses and children of political enemies were encouraged to draw a line between themselves and the victim.

64. That is, Little Mrs.

65. The "four olds," *si jiu*: old ideas, old culture, old customs, and old habits. They were attacked in the Cultural Revolution.

66. Her son, to whom she gave a girl's name to ward off evil spirits.

67. The official residence of Mao Zedong and senior Party leaders in downtown Beijing.

68. The five red classes (*hong wu lei*) were those social groups deemed most revolutionary during the Cultural Revolution: workers, poor and middle peasants, soldiers of the People's Liberation Army (PLA), revolutionary cadres, and revolutionary martyrs.

69. In the Cultural Revolution one's putative economic class (e.g., peasant, worker, petty bourgeoisie) strongly determined one's political fate. *Historical problems* refers to previous political errors or behaviors currently out of favor.

70. That is, in danger of falling in (to political troubles) and melting, too.

71. Private telephones were unheard of for those beneath the level of the CCP elite until the 1980s. Urban residential areas had small huts with a communal telephone, staffed by some older resident appointed by the Neighborhood Committee for each area.

72. He is using classical Confucian terms to say, "If you are unkind to me, then I'll be unkind to you."

73. "Three Family Village" (*sanjiacun*) was a notorious negative example in the Cultural Revolution of three leading Beijing Party intellectuals deemed by Mao to be counterrevolutionary. They were "exposed" in spring 1966 at the start of the Cultural Revolution and used as a model for attacking local counterrevolutionaries. Their leader was Deng Tuo. See Timothy Cheek, *Propaganda and Culture in Mao's China: Deng Tuo and the Intelligentsia* (Oxford: Clarendon Press, 1997).

74. The *Yiguandao* was a famous "secret society" in the nineteenth and twentieth centuries. These semi-illegal groups of young men acted something like gangs or the Mafia do in the United States today.

75. Little Ring is using a distinction made famous by Mao in February 1957: contradictions among the people are to be handled with education; contradictions between the people and the enemy are to be handled with force. Little Ring is making light of this political formulation in his usual cynical way.

76. It is not clear who this man is. The context provided in the play suggests that he was a leader of the Work Teams sent by Liu Shaoqi to Beijing University in the summer of 1966. Little Liben is a member of an analogous team sent to Little Ring's work unit. Since the Work Teams were repudiated by Mao later in 1966, Little Ring is implying that Little Liben is a "local branch" of such "counterrevolutionary" activities.

77. Shi Chuanxiang was a labor hero popularized by the CCP but then denounced in the Cultural Revolution. Little Ring is here mocking the forced political criticism of such hapless victims by applying it to the ridiculous case of neighborhood water delivery.

78. Work Teams were organized by Liu Shaoqi in the early summer of 1966 to handle the disruptions of the Cultural Revolution. Mao reversed Liu's policies by midsummer, and all cadres who had worked in the Work Teams were denounced. The Byzantine politics of the first year of the Cultural Revolution are nicely recounted in Yan and Gao, *Turbulent Decade*.

79. That is, she is pregnant.

80. Volume 12, 1966, issue of *Hong Qi* (Red Flag), the leading theory journal of the CCP. This editorial outlined a further radicalizing of the Cultural Revolution.

81. For the "four olds," see note 11; the "four news" are parallel: new ideas, new culture, new customs, new habits. Red Guards attacked people almost randomly in 1966 and 1967 in the name of enforcing this policy. See Yan and Gao, *Turbulent Decade*, pt. 1.

82. The radical leadership of the Cultural Revolution, known as the Gang of Four—Jiang Qing (Madam Mao), Zhang Chunqiao, Yao Wenyuan, and

Wang Hongwen—was purged on October 8, 1976, about one month after the death of Mao himself on September 7, 1976. After their purge the radicals were called the Gang of Four by the post-Mao leadership.

83. Tangshan, an industrial city between Tianjin and Beijing, was devastated by an earthquake in the summer of 1976. Many people felt it was an omen about Mao's impending death. Such earthquakes traditionally marked the "end of the dynasty." Here it is also used as a political metaphor (like the winds opening act 3), in this case suggesting the damaged nature of the late–Cultural Revolution regime.

84. *Dujuan Shan* (Cuckoo mountain) is one of the ten model "revolutionary operas" championed by Jiang Qing during the Cultural Revolution. This one recounts Mao's glorious exploits in the Anyuan miners' strike in the 1920s.

85. Rationing coupons needed to purchase cloth. On the rationing system, see note 42.

86. Many ordinary people came to present similar petitions to the Beijing government after Deng Xiaoping assumed real power in December 1978. The press was full of such cases into the early 1980s.

87. Er Niu was arrested at the famous "April 5 movement" of 1976, which occurred in Tiananmen Square during the annual Qingming mourning festival. The demonstrations were on behalf of Premier Zhou Enlai, who had died that January, and against the radical leadership around Jiang Qing that sought to diminish his role and policies. The April 5 demonstrations were officially designated as a "counterrevolutionary movement" until the early 1980s.

88. Referring to the spot where the April 5 demonstrations during the Qingming mourning festival were taking place. Little Mrs. is the instrument of the radical leadership for punishing such protests.

89. *Xiang yang yuan* is a term from the Cultural Revolution indicating the political correctness of those compounds or residential courtyards that had followed the policy directives of the day most successfully. The "sun" is Mao Zedong, and the entire metaphor stands for automatic loyalty to Mao's wishes in the fashion of a flower turning toward the sun. Such terms have brought ironic laughter to most Chinese audiences since the early 1980s.

90. A term of respect for Grandma Teng. *Shiniang* refers to the wife of one's teacher—in martial arts or in one's trade; see note 22.

91. *Kongcheng ji* is one of the famous military stratagems of Zhuge Liang, the hero of the popular traditional novel *Three Kingdoms*. *Three Kingdoms* was written by Luo Guanzhong and published in Ming Dynasty. One English translation of the novel is *Three Kingdoms: A Historical Novel* (Berkeley: University of California Press, 1991).

92. Celebrations announcing the arrest of the Gang of Four (Jiang Qing and the ultra-leftist leadership), officially bringing the Cultural Revolution to an end.

93. Hundreds of thousands of youth—mostly Red Guard activists—who had been "sent down to the countryside" returned to Beijing and other major

cities in the years following Mao's death. By 1980 their return had caused a housing crisis.

94. The *pi-pa* is a traditional Chinese stringed instrument that makes a plunking sound like a banjo.

95. By the early 1980s local residents were allowed to set up small free markets (i.e., not state-run enterprises) to provide consumer goods and services.

96. This is a popular tale of Yue Fei, the loyalist general of the Song Dynasty who was purged by political enemies. He stands in post-Mao China as a common metaphor for Premier Zhou Enlai and more generally for all the loyal Party members purged during the Cultural Revolution and rehabilitated in the 1980s.

97. *Cankao xiaoxi* is officially a restricted circulation newspaper, but in the post-Mao period it has been widely available. That Liu Jiaxiang is referring to it rather than the more open papers, such as *People's Daily,* draws our attention to the opening of public information after the Cultural Revolution.

98. A warning to Little Ring that his private business dealings, while approved in the early 1980s, may be subject to political attack in the future. Private entrepreneurship has increased drastically in the fifteen years since this play was first published. For a sense of China in the 1990s, see Michael Dutton, *Streetlife China* (Cambridge: Cambridge University Press, 1998); and Timothy B. Weston and Lionel M. Jensen, eds., *China beyond the Headlines* (Lanham, Md.: Rowman and Littlefield, 2000).

99. China's western desert province some thousand miles from Beijing.

100. Auntie Six is Spring Happiness. Shopkeeper Shi's formality indicates goodwill.

Glossary

Cankao xiaoxi 参考消息
Chaguan 茶馆
Da feng ge 大风歌
da zi bao 大字报
Dujuan shan 杜鹃山
feng shui 风水
Hong deng ji 红灯记
hongqi 红旗
Huo zhe 活着
Hutong jiushijiu 胡同 99
Jiehun jinxing qu 结婚进行曲
jun tong 军统
Kang Youwei 康有为
Kong cheng ji 空城记
lao san jie 老三界
Lao She 老舍
Luan shi nan nu 乱世男女
Mao Dun 茅盾
niang-niang miao 娘娘庙
qi ling jie 七零界
renmin gongshe 人民公社
san jia cun 三家村
Sheng guan tu 升官图
shiniang 师娘
si he yuan 四合院
si jiu 四旧
sixiang jiefang 思想解放
Tan Sitong 谭嗣同
tian jing 天井
tong ling ren 同龄人
Wang Zengqi 汪曾琪
Wan zhu 顽主
wuxu 戊戌
xiang yang yuan 向阳院
xiao jing 孝敬
xi jin zhi 西津志
xiang fang 厢房
yangban xi 样板戏
yin yang tou 阴阳头
zheng fang 正房
zhi qu weihu shan 智取威虎山
zui keai de ren 最可爱的人

Bibliography

A Selection of Works by Li Longyun

"A Song in Winds and Rains" (*Feng yu lou zhong de ge*). Poem. *Chinese Literature* (winter 1972).
There Is a Small Courtyard (*You zhe yang yi ge xiao yuan*). Four-act play. *Heilongjiang Drama*, no. 4 (1979).
Small Well Lane (*Xiaojing hutong*). Five-act play. *Drama Monthly*, no. 5 (1981). This is the text on which our translation is based.
Not Far from the Old Summer Palace (*Zheli bu yuan shi yuanming yuan*). Five-act play. *Harvest*, no. 5 (1982).
The Collapse of Luomahu Kingdom (*Luomahu wangguo de fumo*). Novel. *World*, no. 5 (1985).
Wilderness and Man (*Huangyuan yu ren*). Multi-act play. *Drama Monthly*, no. 11 (1987).
A Collection of Li Longyun's Humor (*Li Longyun youmo duan ju jijin*), *Beijing New Plays*, no. 1 (1987).
Under the Red Banner (*Zeng hongqi xia*). Multi-act play. *New Drama*, no. 7 (1999).
Wilderness and Man: A Collection of Selected Works of Li Longyun (*Huangyuan yu ren: Li Longyun juzuo xuan*). Beijing: China Social Science Publishing House, 1993. This collection includes six major plays and several other writings by Li.
Debates on Small Well Lane (*Xiaojing fengbo lu*). Harbin: Heilongjiang People's Publishing House, 1987. This volume includes the 1985 revised version of *Small Well Lane*, thirty letters from Chen Baichen, as well as many articles concerning the play.

Useful References

Duke, Michael. *Blooming and Contending: Chinese Literature in the Post-Mao Era*. Bloomington: Indiana University Press, 1985.

Goldblatt, Howard, ed. *Worlds Apart: Recent Chinese Writing and Its Audience.* Armonk, N.Y.: M. E. Sharpe, 1998.
Goldman, Merle, Timothy Cheek, and Carol Lee Hamrin, eds. *China's Intellectuals and the State: In Search of a New Relationship.* Cambridge, Mass.: Harvard University Press, 1987.
Joseph, William, Christine Wong, and David Zweig, eds. *New Perspectives on the Cultural Revolution.* Cambridge, Mass.: Harvard University Press, 1991.
Kinkley, Jeffrey, ed. *After Mao: Chinese Literature and Society, 1978–1981.* Cambridge, Mass.: Harvard University Press, 1985.
Knapp, Ronald G. *China's Living Houses: Folk Beliefs, Symbols, and Household Orientation.* Honolulu: University of Hawaii Press, 1999.
Lao She. *Teahouse.* Beijing: Foreign Languages Press, 1980.
Liu, Kang, and Xiaobing Tang, eds. *Politics, Ideology, and Literary Discourse in Modern China: Theoretical Interventions and Cultural Critique.* Durham, N.C., and London: Duke University Press, 1993.
MacFarquhar, Roderick. *Origins of the Cultural Revolution.* Vols. 1–3. New York: Columbia University Press, 1974, 1983, 1997.
Meisner, Maurice. *Mao's China and After.* New York: Free Press, 1986.
Teiwes, Frederick. *Politics and Purges in Mao's China,* 2d ed. Armonk, N.Y.: M. E. Sharpe, 1993.
Wagner, Rudolg G. *The Contemporary Chinese Historical Drama: Four Studies.* Berkeley: University of California Press, 1990.
Wang, Ban. *The Sublime Figure of History.* Stanford: Stanford University Press, 1997.
Wang, Meng. *Bolshevik Salute,* trans. Wendy Larson. Seattle and London: University of Washington Press, 1989.
Widmer, Ellen, and David Der-wei Wang, eds. *From May Fourth to June Fourth: Fiction and Film in Twentieth-Century China.* Cambridge, Mass.: Harvard University Press, 1993.
Yan, Haiping. *Theater and Society: An Anthology of Contemporary Chinese Drama.* Armonk, N.Y.: M. E. Sharpe, 1998.
Yan, Jiaqi, and Gao Gao. *Turbulent Decade: A History of the Cultural Revolution,* ed. and trans. D. W. Y. Kwok. Honolulu: University of Hawaii Press, 1996.
Yang, Rae. *The Spider Eaters: A Memoir of the Cultural Revolution.* Berkeley: University of California Press, 1996.
Zhang, Xinxin, and Sang Ye. *Chinese Lives: An Oral History of Contemporary China,* eds. and trans. W. J. F. Jenner and Delia Davin. New York: Pantheon Books, 1987.
Zhang, Xudong. *Chinese Modernism in the Era of Reform.* Durham, N.C.: Duke University Press, 1997.
Zheng, Shiping. *Party vs. State in Post–1949 China: The Institutional Dilemma.* New York: Cambridge University Press, 1997.